DECODING THE MYSTERIES OF

HEAVEN'S
WAR ROOM

Other Books by Jennifer LeClaire

DECODING THE MYSTERIES OF

HEAVEN'S WAR ROOM

21 HEAVENLY STRATEGIES FOR
POWERFUL PRAYER AND TRIUMPHANT WARFARE

JENNIFER LECLAIRE

DESTINY IMAGE® PUBLISHERS, INC.
P.O. Box 310, Shippensburg, PA 17257-0310
"Promoting Inspired Lives."

This book and all other Destiny Image and Destiny Image Fiction books are available at Christian bookstores and distributors worldwide.

Cover design by Eileen Rockwell.

For more information on foreign distributors, call 717-532-3040.

Reach us on the Internet: www.destinyimage.com.

ISBN 13 TP: 978-0-7684-5910-4

ISBN 13 eBook: 978-0-7684-5911-1

ISBN 13 HC: 978-0-7684-5913-5

ISBN 13 LP: 978-0-7684-5912-8

For Worldwide Distribution, Printed in the U.S.A.

1 2 3 4 5 6 7 8 / 25 24 23 22 21

ACKNOWLEDGMENTS

Many thanks to my prophetic warriors at Awakening House of Prayer in Ft. Lauderdale and my Awakening Prayer Hubs leaders around the world for fighting the good fight. I'm grateful that we are in this together. Thanks to Bishop Bill Hamon and my Christian International family for being prophetic warriors who model the way for me and many others. Thanks also to Larry Sparks and the team at Destiny Image who understand the stakes of the battle we're in and follow the leadership of the Holy Spirit in their publishing ministry.

CONTENTS

CHAPTER 1

WHEN

MYSTERIES BECOME REVELATIONS

G od will unlock mysteries to you, and when you pen these mysteries they will become revelations." Decades ago, a notable apostle prophesied those words over me. At the time, my ear heard but my eyes could not see the significance of the utterance. My natural mind could not comprehend the deeper meaning of the prophetic words, but my spirit understood it was a weighty prophecy.

Nothing happened. Not immediately. I received no revelation. I apprehended no mystery. I experienced no encounters. That prophetic word was a seed that would not yield its harvest for many years to come. Indeed, the promise was so far away, at times, I actually forgot about it. Maybe you can relate. Maybe you have a few prophetic words in a drawer or on a shelf.

Then one day, nearly twenty years later, the Holy Spirit reminded me of that prophecy. Yes, He reminded me after an epic vision of the war room in heaven that would mark me—an epic vision I meditated on for over a year before I sat down to release *The Vision*. As I put my pen to paper, many mysteries hidden in this epic vision were unraveled, one by one, by the Holy Spirit. And I received practical application I will share in great detail in the pages that follow.

This epic vision, along with other prophetic encounters and divine downloads printed in this book, will help you understand God's plans and purposes in the earth in this hour and the hour to come—and encourage you to take your place in God's storyline. The epic vision starts in a war room, but before we can get to the war room we need to gain a revelation of the realm I entered to receive the mysteries that became revelations.

See, the rooms in heaven are one aspect of the mysteries of God. Few people have seen them and fewer talk about them. But the rooms in heaven are just as much a reality as heaven itself. The rooms in heaven are part of the mystical realm of the seer dimension. (You can learn more about this in my book, *The Seer Dimensions*.) In order to get the most out of this epic vision and other prophetic encounters I will share, it's important to understand this truth: God is unlocking ancient mysteries in this hour through dreams and visions, angelic encounters—and His still small voice.

ENTERING MYSTICAL REALMS

Although some modern-day self-proclaimed mystics have introduced error to the Body of Christ, mysticism is not itself an error. It's a biblical concept. We must be careful not to reject treasure chests of biblical truth early church mystics left behind because of a few heretics. Paul the apostle walked in the mystical realm and his ability to expound on the mysteries of the gospel was the result. Paul said God made known to Him mysteries by revelation so that he could share knowledge with the church (see Eph. 3:2-6). Paul wrote two-thirds of the New Testament by way of direct revelation and unlocked many mysteries in the process. Nevertheless, Paul barely scratched the surface of the mystical realm.

The English word *mystery* in Ephesians 3:3 comes from the Greek word *musterion*. According to *The KJV New Testament Greek Lexicon*, it means, "hidden thing, secret, mystery, generally mysteries, religious secrets, confided only to the initiated and not to ordinary mortals, a hidden or secret thing, not obvious to the understanding, a hidden purpose or counsel, the secret counsels which govern God in dealing with the righteous, which are hidden from ungodly and wicked men but plain to the godly in rabbinic writings, it denotes the mystic or hidden sense, a saying, an image or form seen in a vision, dream."

Bethel's Bill Johnson taught me the ability to embrace mystery is what attracts revelation. We often brush over what we don't readily understand. But biblical curiosity and spiritual hunger—persistently asking, seeking, and knocking on the door of the secret place—opens doors of reward. Be assured, God is a rewarder of those who diligently seek Him (see Heb. 11:6). I believe the Holy Spirit not only shows us things to come, but shows us things that were and will be one day. Some of these are mysteries.

YOU CAN ACCESS MYSTERIES

Jesus wants His disciples to know the mysteries of the Kingdom of heaven. This is not my opinion. He clearly said to His disciples, "It has been given to you to know the mysteries of the kingdom of heaven" (Matt. 13:11). *The Passion Translation* puts it this way, "You've been given the intimate experience of insight into the hidden truths and mysteries of the realm of heaven's kingdom."

We have to press into the mystical and ecstatic realms through study of the Word and prayer, often contemplative prayer. Contemplative prayer is an ancient Christian practice that dates all the way back to the early church and even to the life of King David. The psalms give proof of David's contemplative prayer life. David wrote, "I will meditate on Your precepts, and contemplate Your ways" (Ps. 119:15).

Contemplation is "a concentration on spiritual things as a form of private devotion or a state of mystical awareness of God's being," according to *Merriam-Webster*'s dictionary. It's an act of considering with attention, the act of regarding steadily, intention and expectation. Contemplative prayer is a thoughtful practice where you focus on the Word of God to the point where you drown out other thoughts, feelings, and temporal distractions. You are focusing on the Father, Son, and Holy Spirit within you rather than the Father, Son, and Holy Spirit outside of you. God's voice becomes clearer through this practice.

The realms of contemplative prayer and Christian mysticism are largely misunderstood, and error can creep in if we are not rooted in the Word. But the reality is the Word has plenty to say about this dimension, which includes the rooms in heaven. The Bible calls us stewards of the mysteries of God (see 1 Cor. 4:1). We can't steward something we haven't unlocked. Mysteries become revelation as

God opens the eyes of our heart so we can see what we could not see before—things that were there all along.

Proverbs 25:2 reveals: "It is the glory of God to conceal a matter, but the glory of kings is to search out a matter." And Deuteronomy 29:29 says, "The secret things belong to the Lord our God, but those things which are revealed belong to us and to our children forever, that we may do all the words of this law." Jeremiah 33:3 instructs us: "Call to Me, and I will answer you, and show you great and mighty things, which you do not know."

Ultimately, the wisdom of the Christian mystics from hundreds of years ago—such as Teresa of Avila, Francis of Assisi, Hildegard of Bingen, John of the Cross, and Julian of Norwich—is priceless. Christian mysticism is guidance for living in the love of God, according to Carl McColman, author of *The Little Book of Christian Mysticism.* McColman writes:

> God does not merely love us lavishly and joyfully, like a mother loves her child. Yes, of course, God does that, although thanks to centuries of religious misguidance, many people are blind even to this basic spiritual truth. But the mystics remind us that it gets even better than being loved unconditionally: the heart of the mystery is not just *being loved,* but *being love.*[1]

We will see mystery after mystery unravel one day—on the other side of glory—including a fuller understanding of the rooms in heaven. But sometimes, the Lord gives us glimpses of those rooms now. I saw a room with the books written about the lives of God's servants. This was the first room in the spirit I ever saw, and one that would set the stage to move deeper beyond the veil.

REVELATIONS RECORDED AND LOST

I was on my face during worship at Awakening House of Prayer, the headquarters for our Ft. Lauderdale church and global prayer movement. In this vision, I saw a veil rip open from the top to bottom. I am unsure if God Himself ripped open the veil or if the angels in heaven dismantled the visual barrier between the realms of heaven and earth.

As I peered behind the veil, I saw a long walkway with bookshelves and tables on either side. It looked like a lonely path where few had traveled over the ages. At first, I couldn't see anyone on the path. What I could see were books—many, many books. Rows and rows of books. Finally, my attention was drawn to a man walking down the open path with a magnifying glass, almost like an investigator. He was looking at the scrolls.

The man was examining the fine print, looking closer at things others seemed to have missed. He would open one book and peer into it as if searching for something in particular. He would move on to several books, continuing his careful search, before the vision concluded. When I asked the Lord what the man was looking into, I suddenly had a knowing in my spirit that these books were full of mysteries that became revelations to generations past—revelations recorded and lost.

I understood these books of mysteries contain revelations angels long to look into. As I continued to lie on my face, the worship music in the background faintly dim, I understood some of these books contained mysteries of the blood and mysteries of angels that were unlocked to the mystics of the early church and are waiting for a new generation to press into.

There were also books with mysteries that have yet been hidden that God wants to release in this generation. Some of those mysteries have to do with spiritual warfare, deliverance, and demonology. We live in an age in which the enemy knows his time is not only short—but quickly running out. He discerns the signs of the times as well as any of us. He's been watching for thousands of years.

Before I got up off the floor, the Holy Spirit said to me:

> *Who will walk through the open veil? Who will investigate the books and scrolls of the past generations and unlock ancient revelation for the present day? Who will pay the price to see? Who will clear out the eyes of the world's images and see heavenly images? There's a price to pay to see into the deep things of God.*

This book is the firstfruits of that vision. Mysteries became revelations to me even in the process of writing. My prayer is the Holy Spirit will solve mysteries that strike curiosity in your heart as you read the pages of this book.

NOTE

1. Carl McColman, *The Little Book of Christian Mysticism* (Charlottesville, VA: Hampton Roads Publishing Company, Inc., 2018), 2.

CHAPTER 2

THE MYSTERY
OF THE TORN VEIL

When Jesus died on the cross, the veil of the temple was torn in two from top to bottom (see Mark 15:38). In that moment, those who believe in Christ were given the ability to see behind the veil. What is the veil? The Greek word for *veil* is *kalupto*. It means "to hide, veil, to hinder the knowledge of a thing," according to *The KJV New Testament Greek Lexicon*. *Merriam-Webster*'s dictionary defines *veil* as something used to cover, provide, obscure, or conceal.

That's an interesting definition, as it means when the veil is torn mysteries are revealed—knowledge is no longer hindered. Except, that is, by the enemy of your spirit. For thousands upon thousands of years, there has been (and is still) a battle for the spiritual eyes of mankind. Adam and Eve saw in the spirit until the fall of man, and God has been trying to restore our vision ever since.

From Second Corinthians 4:4 we understand, "For the god of this world has blinded the unbelievers' minds [that they should not discern the truth], preventing them from seeing the illuminating light of the Gospel of the glory of Christ (the Messiah), Who is the Image and Likeness of God" (AMPC). And Jesus said, "I assure you, most solemnly I tell you, that unless a person is born again (anew, from above), he cannot ever see (know, be acquainted with, and experience) the kingdom of God" (John 3:3 AMPC).

When your human spirit was born again, your eyes were legally opened to God's Kingdom. You have the ability to see behind the veil whatever God chooses to show you. The seer anointing is part of our God-given discernment. It's time for a generation of seeing people to move, live, and have their being in Christ with spiritual eyes wide open. I pray this book will stir your seer gift and challenge you to see where your eyes have not gone before.

As I write in my book, *Seer Activations*, our heavenly Father is known as "the God who sees" (Gen. 16:13). Just as He is everywhere all the time, He sees everything, everywhere, all the time. Nothing escapes His sight (see Heb. 4:13). You were created in the image of God. You are a spirit, you have a soul, and you live in a body. Therefore, at your core, you are a seeing spirit. And you have a Christ-bought right to see into the spirit dimensions with your spiritual eyes.

SEEING BEHIND THE VEIL

The veil between heaven and earth still exists, but it's getting thinner. In other words, it's getting easier to see through the veil and into the spirit. Modern mystics are developing seer focus to home in on what God wants to show them. Encounters behind the veil do not come through striving but through seeking God and, often, waiting in silence. Other times they come suddenly, even at inconvenient times. (I write about the silent dimension in my book *The Seer Dimensions*.)

Hebrews 6:19 speaks of a hope that serves as a strong and trustworthy anchor for our souls. That hope paves the way into His presence behind the veil, since we go there by faith and faith is the substance of things hoped for (see Heb. 11:1). *The Passion Translation* puts it this way: "Our anchor of hope is fastened to the mercy seat which sits in the heavenly realm beyond the sacred threshold, and where Jesus..." (Heb. 6:19-20 TPT). This hope reaches beyond the curtain into the Throne Room. Let that sink in. Jesus Himself is our hope and gives us the measure of faith to follow Him behind the veil. *MacLaren's Expositions* writes:

> A veil is but a thin partition. We can hear the voices on the other side of a woollen curtain, we can catch the gleams of light through it, A touch will draw it aside. So we float in the midst of that solemn unseen present which is to us the future; and all the brightest and grandest objects of the Christian man's anticipation have a present existence and are real; just on the other side of that thin curtain that parts us from them.

One of the mysteries Paul unraveled by revelation is this: When we turn to the Lord, the veil is taken away. When the veil is removed, we can behold the glory of the Lord (see 2 Cor. 3:16-18). Our legal position is seated in heavenly places with Christ Jesus even now (see Eph. 2:4-5). We are seated behind the veil, even if we don't yet see behind the veil. But, again, the veil is growing thinner as the Second Coming of Christ approaches. We're seeing more people encountering heaven, hell, and receiving profound visual revelation.

"Mystery is one of the greatest lures of romance and intimacy. The magnetism draws us, woos us, even propels us to find what we have yet to experience, to find what our heart knows is there," John Paul Jackson wrote in *7 Days Behind the Veil*. "We can sense it. Our logic argues against it, but the mystery becomes so much our desire that in the end, we pursue it with everything we have, unmindful of the cost."[1]

In my *Seer's Dictionary*, I help readers explore the concept of hidden—which is the essence of mystery. The *Seer's Dictionary* defines hidden as "beyond unseen, something hidden is purposely kept from view." As the veil grows thinner, God is revealing things hidden from understanding, hidden snares of the enemy, hidden treasures, and more. One of the keys to exploring the mystical realms is having God's words, precepts, and principles hidden in your heart (see Ps. 119:11) and staying hidden in Christ (see Col 3:3).

A HUMAN THIRST FOR THE DIVINE

In his classic book *The Pursuit of God*, A.W. Tozer penned some words we need to embrace in this generation. Words that have stirred my heart to the point that I was stirred in my spirit to the point of shivering from the inside out.

> With the veil removed by the rending of Jesus' flesh, with nothing on God's side to prevent us from entering,

why do we tarry without? Why do we consent to abide all our days just outside the Holy of Holies and never enter at all to look upon God? We hear the Bridegroom say, "Let me see thy countenance, let me hear thy voice; for sweet is thy voice and thy countenance is comely." We sense that the call is for us, but still we fail to draw near, and the years pass and we grow old and tired in the outer courts of the tabernacle. What doth hinder us?

The answer usually given, simply that we are "cold," will not explain all the facts. There is something more serious than coldness of heart, something that may be back of that coldness and be the cause of its existence. What is it? What but the presence of a veil in our hearts? A veil not taken away as the first veil was, but which remains there still shutting out the light and hiding the face of God from us. It is the veil of our fleshly fallen nature living on, unjudged within us, uncrucified and unrepudiated.

It is the close-woven veil of the self-life which we have never truly acknowledged, of which we have been secretly ashamed, and which for these reasons we have never brought to the judgment of the cross. It is not too mysterious, this opaque veil, nor is it hard to identify. We have but to look in our own hearts and we shall see it there, sewn and patched and repaired it may be, but there nevertheless, an enemy to our lives and an effective block to our spiritual progress.

This veil is not a beautiful thing and it is not a thing about which we commonly care to talk, but I am addressing the thirsting souls who are determined to follow God, and I know they will not turn back because the way leads temporarily through the blackened hills. The urge of God within them will assure their continuing the pursuit. They will face the facts however unpleasant and endure the cross for the joy set before them. So I am bold to mane the threads out of which this inner veil is woven. It is woven of the fine threads of the self-life, the hyphenated sins of the human spirit. They are not something we do, they are something we are, and therein lies both their subtlety and their power.[2]

THE ROOMS WITHIN

I had an extraordinary vision that taught me we often need to explore the rooms within before gaining access to visuals of the rooms in heaven. I experienced this vision while sitting in my prayer chair in silence, contemplating the goodness and beauty of God.

Suddenly, I saw myself walking toward a magnificent castle. As I walked through the middle of the castle, it rolled up and went inside my spirit. I heard the Lord say, "The Kingdom of God is within you. Everything you need is within you. All the resources you require are within you. You don't even have to pull it down from heaven. It is within you. Speak it out of your mouth and you will see it. Christ in you, the hope of glory. The riches in glory in Christ are within you."

When I experienced this vision, I had never heard of Teresa of Avila's book *The Interior Castle*. In it, she speaks of seven stages of union with God. To move from stage to stage you are moving from room to room within this inner castle. This is an exercise of contemplative prayer. Teresa writes, "Since God has given it such great dignity, permit it to wander at will through the rooms of the castle, from the lowest to the highest. Let it not force itself to remain for very long in the same mansion, even that of self knowledge."[3]

The reality is, the Kingdom of God is within you, which could be better translated "among you" (Luke 17:21 AMPC). But the flesh veils this reality. God is omnipresent and His Kingdom of God is all around us. It's not difficult to believe God can and even wants to show us aspects of our real home. As citizens of heaven, we should be spiritually intrigued by this invisible Kingdom where our supernatural King dwells. God is a God of rooms, which we will explore in the next chapter.

BECOMING FULLY AWAKE

I am convinced more than ever that many of us walk around half asleep with hurry sickness that overwhelms our souls and dulls the sensitivity of our spirit. I recently saw something in Luke 9:23-36 I never saw before. Read the passage with me and I'll explain.

> *Then He said to them all, "If anyone desires to come after Me, let him deny himself, and take up his cross daily, and follow Me. For whoever desires to save his life will lose it, but whoever loses his life for My sake will save it. For what profit is it to a man if he gains the whole world, and is himself destroyed or lost? For whoever is ashamed of Me and My words, of him the Son of Man will be ashamed when He*

comes in His own glory, and in His Father's, and of the holy angels. But I tell you truly, there are some standing here who shall not taste death till they see the kingdom of God."

Now it came to pass, about eight days after these sayings, that He took Peter, John, and James and went up on the mountain to pray. As He prayed, the appearance of His face was altered, and His robe became white and glistening. And behold, two men talked with Him, who were Moses and Elijah, who appeared in glory and spoke of His decease which He was about to accomplish at Jerusalem. But Peter and those with him were heavy with sleep; and when they were fully awake, they saw His glory and the two men who stood with Him. Then it happened, as they were parting from Him, that Peter said to Jesus, "Master, it is good for us to be here; and let us make three tabernacles: one for You, one for Moses, and one for Elijah"—not knowing what he said.

While he was saying this, a cloud came and overshadowed them; and they were fearful as they entered the cloud. And a voice came out of the cloud, saying, "This is My beloved Son. Hear Him!" When the voice had ceased, Jesus was found alone. But they kept quiet, and told no one in those days any of the things they had seen.

A GLORIOUS REVELATION

This is one of the most glorious revelations of Christ in the Bible—and it's noteworthy that it came right after Jesus instructed His disciples to pick up their cross and follow Him. Jesus was calling His followers to crucify the flesh, as He was getting ready to allow Roman soldiers to crucify Him at Calvary.

Although Jesus invited John, James, and Peter up to this mountain, presumably to pray, they could not stay awake. The Bible says they were heavy with sleep. It wasn't until they were fully awake—not half awake, but fully awake—that they saw the appearance of His face altered and His robe glistening white. It wasn't until they were fully awake that they saw His glory.

How did they suddenly become fully awake? It takes God to wake us up to the things of the spirit. We can pursue, and our spirit is willing but our flesh is weak (see Matt. 26:41). It takes God's glory to wake us up to His glory. While meditating on the passage in Luke 9, I had a vision where I saw Peter waking up. He was rubbing his eyes, almost in disbelief at what he was seeing. He was disoriented.

What woke him up? It was the glory of God radiating off Jesus that woke up Peter, James, and John. They were never the same. The encounter changed them. That's what the glory does. But there's more: When they were fully awake—awakened by God—John, James, and Peter saw behind the veil as Jesus encountered Moses and Elijah.

I pray this book wakes you up to the reality of the realm of the spirit as you explore a little-revealed topic of the rooms in heaven. But the greater purpose of this book is to help you understand what the Lord is doing in the end times. There is a war room in heaven.

NOTES

1. John Paul Jackson, *7 Days Behind the Veil* (North Sutton, NH: Streams Publishing House, 2006), 39.

2. A.W. Tozer *The Pursuit of God* (Harrisburg, PA: Christian Publications, Inc., 2008), 43-45.

3. St. Teresa of Avila, *The Interior Castle* (Charlotte, NC: Saint Benedict Press, 2011), 18.

CHAPTER 3

THE MYSTERY

OF HEAVEN'S SECRET ROOMS

Just behind the veil, I saw one of the many rooms in heaven. Yes, there are many rooms in heaven. Most believers haven't meditated on this spiritual reality, but Jesus gave His disciples insight into these heavenly rooms while He walked the earth. Jesus told His disciples there are "many rooms" in His Father's house. There are even secret rooms few see. At least one of those rooms contains hidden knowledge. I saw it.

Jesus said emphatically: "There are many rooms in my Father's house. I wouldn't tell you this, unless it was true. I am going there to prepare a place for each of you" (John 14:2 CEV). *The Message* puts it this way, "There is plenty of room for you in my Father's home. If that weren't so, would I have told you that I'm on my way to get a room ready for you?"

We know Jesus went ahead of us to prepare a place for us, but beyond the rooms reserved for Christians who go on to glory, there are other rooms in heaven. The Bible leaves record for the generations to explore, and many believers throughout the ages have seen some of these rooms in the spirit.

Samuel Rutherford, a 17th century Scottish pastor, wrote, "Go up beforehand and see your lodging. Look through all your Father's rooms in heaven; in your Father's house are many dwelling-places. Men take a sight of lands ere they buy them. I know Christ hath made the bargain already: but be kind to the house ye are going to, and see it often."[1]

ROOMS BY DIVINE DESIGN

God is a God of purpose—and He is also a God of rooms. A room is a space sufficient or available for something or a partitioned part of the inside of a building, according to *Merriam-Webster*'s dictionary. You've heard of multipurpose rooms—rooms that can be used for many different things. But it seems the rooms in heaven are purposed for specific activities.

Indeed, we see God-ordained rooms throughout Scripture. When Jehovah called Noah to build an ark, He told him to make rooms for the different animals (see Gen. 6:14). Several prophets received first-hand visions of the throne room in heaven, which are vividly outlined in Scripture. One day all creation will bow to the majesty of God's throne in this awesome room.

King David had it on his heart to build a house for the Lord, but God told the man of war he could not build a house for His name because he had shed blood. With that, God assured David his son Solomon would build His house and His courts (see 1 Chron. 28:2-6). When God gave David the design for the temple, it had clearly designated rooms. The temple Solomon built represents heaven's house on earth.

> *Then David gave Solomon the plans for the Temple and its surroundings, including the entry room, the storerooms, the upstairs rooms, the inner rooms, and the inner sanctuary— which was the place of atonement. David also gave Solomon all the plans he had in mind for the courtyards of the Lord's Temple, the outside rooms, the treasuries, and the rooms for the gifts dedicated to the Lord. The king also gave Solomon the instructions concerning the work of the various divisions of priests and Levites in the Temple of the Lord. And he gave specifications for the items in the Temple that were to be used for worship* (1 Chronicles 28:11-13 NLT).

Notice all the rooms—entry rooms, storerooms, upper rooms, inner rooms, outside rooms, and rooms for gifts dedicated to the Lord. First Kings gives more detail about how particular God was about the rooms and their dimensions. The entry room at the front of the temple was 30 feet wide, running across the entire width of the temple. There was a complex of rooms against the outer walls of the temple, all the way around the sides and rear of the building.

Of course, the Holy of Holies was the most important room. That translates to the throne room in heaven. Nothing about the rooms in heaven is random. There is a purpose for each one, and each one is necessary.

THE MYSTERY OF ROOMS IN HEAVEN

Just as the whole world could not possibly make room for the chronicles of Christ's work on the earth (see John 21:25), the Bible doesn't contain documentation on every room in heaven. The biblically curious will pray in their upper room in expectation of discovering more about the Kingdom of heaven. We can't make God show us the rooms in heaven, but God is a rewarder of those who diligently seek Him (see Heb. 11:6). Seeking God and His Kingdom first opens our spirits to see more of what the Father is doing.

Pulpit Commentary writes: "Heaven is a large place; its possibilities transcend your imagination and exceed your charity." Surely, there are many rooms in heaven—including rooms prepared just for believers who pass into glory. Jesus said, "If it were not so, I would have told you" (John 14:2).

Jesus is not a man that He should lie or the son of man that He should repent—and He is the Door into heavenly rooms. The Holy Spirit is One who leads us and guides us into the rooms in heaven as Jesus wills. Put another way, it's by the invitation of Christ and the leadership of the Holy Spirit that we see the rooms in heaven. These rooms are kept secret to many, but He shows them to some. If you can't see them, know by faith in the Word that they exist. *Coffman's Commentaries on the Bible* offers:

> Speculations regarding the "many [rooms]" are fruitless. It is enough for us to know that they are indeed a reality, despite their existence beyond the perimeter of mortal vision. The souls which are of the faith of Jesus Christ

shall truly inherit the upper and better habitations, and the Lord is even now preparing for the reception of the redeemed in the eternal world.[2]

DISCOVERING HEAVEN'S SECRETS

John Paul Jackson once told TBN:

> I believe if we will humble ourselves before the hand of the Mighty God, that He will give us secrets that no one has heard about before. He will open rooms in heaven to show us things that we've never understood before. He is waiting to release a level of revelation, release experiences in Him that He has not been able to release. Because if He can't trust us in the little things, how in the world is He going to trust us in the greater things?[3]

God is the revealer of secrets (see Dan. 2:47). Deuteronomy 29:29 tells us, "The secret things belong to the Lord our God, but those things which are revealed belong to us and to our children forever, that we may do all the words of this law." David revealed by the Spirit of God that Jehovah reveals His secrets to those who fear Him (see Ps. 25:14).

Heaven's secrets are more readily revealed to those who dwell in the secret place. Of course, most Christians are familiar with Psalm 91:1: "He who dwells in the secret place of the Most High shall abide under the shadow of the Almighty." Those who visit the secret place will be touched and receive revelation, but those who abide there have a different experience to share. The Bible speaks of the secret counsel of God (see Prov. 3:32), the secret of God's presence (see Ps. 31:20), the secret of the Kingdom of God (see Mark 4:11), secrets of wisdom (see Job 11:6), and more.

When you abide in the secret place, you position yourself for God to whisper His secrets to your heart and show you the unseen realm. The secret place is about more than protection—much more. The secret place is where you worship within the veil, living a life of constant communion with him, as *Benson's Commentary* puts it. God has made His abode in you, but it's up to you to abide in Him.

A HEAVENLY INVITATION

This invitation to the secret place, technically, is open to all believers. But few will choose to live in such close fellowship with God that the desires of the world do not sway them. Few choose it because the fire burns. You discover the secret place by an inward walk. Seventeenth century Spanish Christian mystic Miguel de Molinos, who sparked a religious revival known as Quietism, writes:

> By not speaking, desiring, nor reasoning, we reach the central place of the inward walk—that place where God speaks to our inward man. It is there that God communicates Himself to our spirit; and there, in the inmost depths of our being, He teaches us Himself. He guides us to this place where He alone speaks His most secret

and hidden heart. You must enter into this through all silence if you would hear the Divine Voice within you.[4]

Brother Lawrence, the 17th century monk whose personal letters make up a volume called *The Practice of the Presence of God*, understood this reality. Brother Lawrence taught us to intentionally keep our hearts turned toward Him and to occupy ourselves with knowing God. Ultimately, it's about cultivating friendship with God. Like you, God shares His secrets with His friends. *The Treasury of David* commentary offers:

> Those who through rich grace obtain unusual and continuous communion with God, so as to abide in Christ and Christ in them, become possessors of rare and special benefits, which are missed by those who follow afar off, and grieve the Holy Spirit of God. Into the secret place those only come who know the love of God in Christ Jesus, and those only dwell there to whom to live is Christ. To them the veil is rent, the mercy-seat is revealed, the covering cherubs are manifest, and the awful glory of the Most High is apparent.

God's secret place is His heart. There's no map. There's no formula. But there is the leadership of the Holy Spirit. I heard the Holy Spirit say:

> Will you meet Me in the secret place? It's just under the shadow of His wings. There you will find your fortress, your strong tower. It's a safe place where you are shielded from the warfare that tries to distract you from

the beating of My heart and the words that I speak to you. Will you meet Me in that dwelling place? I am waiting for you there, to share wisdom and revelation in the knowledge of Jesus. Just close your eyes and ask Me to take you there now, and where I am you will be. I'm waiting....[5]

SECRET ROOMS IN HEAVEN

The Holy Spirit showed secret rooms in heaven. The concept is akin to hidden rooms in a home. You may have seen such hidden rooms in movies, where false walls give entrance to secret rooms. Even as I sit writing this, I saw a hand reaching out beckoning me to a secret room.

At first, the light was bright and I was disoriented. In this secret room, which appeared to be a storage room, I saw innovations from past generations. These were innovations at which many marveled when they were first revealed. But these innovations have since been disregarded or taken for granted in a modern age. These innovations appeared to be antiques. Some of them were rusty because they hadn't been used in many years.

I began to hear the Lord speak about treasures old and treasures new—new wine and old wine. He explained there's wisdom from the past that will propel many into the future and hope God has for them, but some are too busy chasing the new revelation rather than considering ancient revelations. Many despise the days and ways of the past, even when they are the ways of the Ancient of Days.

When I looked on one side of the room, I looked at the antiques—the innovation of the past. The dominant image was of a plow. When I looked to the other side of the room, I saw modern technology—space technology—and rockets launching into the sky. Although God used natural antiques and modern vehicles, this revelation applies to the things of the spirit. Those who have ears to hear what the Spirit of God is saying to the church, let them hear.

The Lord said, "There are many secret rooms that saints from generations gone by have peered into and have received the joys of. But the new generation must allow Me to do the work in their soul to earn the privilege of entering into and seeing the deep things of God. This next generation will be marked as one that pulls treasures from the old and from the new—that doesn't disregard the glory of the old wineskin in order to embrace a new wineskin but itself will become a vessel that is ageless and timeless and moves with My Spirit." Selah.

OPENING THE TREASURE CHEST

After the vision, I immediately remembered the words of my first mentor. She prophesied over me that I would bring forth treasures old and new. Being young in the Lord at that time, I had no idea what she meant. I do now. I believe now she was prophesying over a generation. Her prophecy was based on Matthew 13:52: "Every student of the Scriptures who becomes a disciple in the kingdom of heaven is like someone who brings out new and old treasures from the storeroom" (CEV). This is one of those Scriptures I had to press into. The Amplified Bible, Classic Edition puts it this way:

Therefore every teacher and interpreter of the Sacred Writings who has been instructed about and trained for the kingdom of heaven and has become a disciple is like a householder who brings forth out of his storehouse treasure that is new and [treasure that is] old [the fresh as well as the familiar].

The struck me. The fresh as well as the familiar. There are treasures—revelations poured out many, many generations ago—that were familiar to the mystics of the day but when re-revealed are fresh for our day. If we will take the time to dig in Scripture and pray, we will find them. I appreciate *The Passion Translation* of this verse:

Every scholar of the Scriptures, who is instructed in the ways of heaven's kingdom realm, is like a wealthy home owner with his house filled with treasures both new and old. And he knows how and when to bring them out to show others.

The International Standard Version of this verse speaks of a treasure chest. We know the Kingdom of heaven itself is like a treasure hidden in a field (see Matt. 13:44). There are revelations of the Kingdom—including but beyond rooms in heaven—waiting to be discovered. Indeed, God has many things laid up in store sealed up among His treasures (see Deut. 32:34).

We begin to find access to these treasures when we understand and subscribe to Job 23:12: "I have not departed from the commandment of His lips; I have treasured the words of His mouth more than my necessary food." The psalmist said, "I rejoice at Your word as one who finds great treasure" (Ps. 119:162). God promises in Isaiah, "I will give you the treasures of darkness and hidden riches of secret places" (Isa. 45:3).

SOMETHING OLD, SOMETHING NEW

For years, Jesus' parables of the new mantle and the new wineskin have troubled me. There's so much talk about new mantles and new wine, but there is little appreciation for the mantles and the wine of the pioneers, forerunners, mystics, visionaries, prophets, and seers who dug wells from which we are now drinking. We don't have to start from scratch. We can benefit from the mantles and wine—the revelations and mysteries—past generations left behind. In Matthew 9:16-17, Jesus said:

> *No one puts a piece of unshrunk cloth on an old garment; for the patch pulls away from the garment, and the tear is made worse. Nor do they put new wine into old wineskins, or else the wineskins break, the wine is spilled, and the wineskins are ruined. But they put new wine into new wineskins, and both are preserved.*

Jesus never said to throw away the old mantle or the old wineskin. In fact, He was concerned about preserving the old mantle and the old wineskin. The "new cloth" was actually speaking of cloth that had not been through the fuller's hand. In the original Greek, it means "rude, undressed, not fulled." *Barnes' Notes on the Bible* suggests if the new, unprepared cloth was applied to an old garment, it would damage the old garment.

What does this mean? In our era of Christianity, we're seeing many "new" revelations. Some of those revelations are pure and holy. Others are damaging to the divine truth revealed in past generations. These damaging revelations often come from unprepared vessels who have not been through the fuller or, as it were, the fire that purifies. God's word is purified seven times (see Ps. 12:6). That means revelation that comes from the throne room is pure and holy—and should be treated as such. Some try to attach their newfangled revelations to ancient truths and, in doing so, tear down instead of building up the Body of Christ.

God does not want us to give the old mantles to Salvation Army or pour the old wine down the proverbial drain. Some of the best, most expensive wine is old wine—aged wine. This brings me back to Matthew 13:52: "Every teacher of religious law who becomes a disciple in the Kingdom of Heaven is like a homeowner who brings from his storeroom new gems of truth as well as old" (NLT).

WALKING THE ANCIENT PATHS

There's something about walking down the ancient paths. In this era of Christianity, God is saying the same thing to us as Jeremiah prophesied to Israel in his day: "Stand by the ways and see, and ask for the old paths, where the good way is, and walk in it; then you will find rest for your souls" (Jer. 6:16). Rest leads us to embrace mysteries that become revelation. The mystics unlocked depths of intimacy that gave them a seemingly open invitation to revelation upon revelation.

Many are looking for the new revelation, but the "now" revelation is just as often an ancient revelation. Present-day truth is often discovered along the ancient paths. When you rest in the Ancient of Days, you will find revelation on those ancient—or everlasting—paths. You will find understanding of ancient matters on the old, godly way. The ancient heights will become your possession.

Every time I visit Singapore, I get a renewed worldview. It's as if the spirit realm opens up to me and I see with greater clarity. I do not know why, other than that God has opened a portal there and has reserved a place for me in the open heaven. Some years ago when I was in Singapore, the Lord released angels of fire to accompany me—and they haven't left me.

In 2018, it was a little more intense. I woke up on my first morning in Singapore with the realization that there were angels and demons in my room. I felt the presence of God, but also felt a war in the spirit. I knew the Holy Spirit was trying to show me something, but there was a battle going on. That battle manifested in the natural with all forms of distractions. I had to press through to receive from the Lord what He had ordained for me that morning.

ANCIENT ANGELS OF REVELATION

After pressing through the battle and quieting my soul, I heard the Lord say:

> *Ancient angels from the company of revelation are going to visit those in this hour who have been experiencing dreams and visions they do not comprehend and cannot understand. I have released companies of revelation angels to expound and explain those deeper truths that*

many could not bear and the mysteries that have so far only been partially unlocked to a few over the ages.

I am releasing these angels with a word of caution to My people: satan disguises himself as an angel of light. Stick close to Me, closer than you have ever drawn, and you will avoid deception and enter into a deeper mode of revelation in your daily walk. The unknown will become known in layers and degrees as you demonstrate consistency in the spirit. I am bringing My seers and prophetic people into a new dimension of the revelatory realm where mind cannot comprehend, but angels can explain.

Just as I sent angels to Daniel and John to bring understanding of what they were seeing, I am dispatching angels on assignment to bring understanding to those who have been crying out for accurate interpretations of things they see and hear as they lay on their bed or as they walk through their days. I am dispatching angels on assignment to bring "aha" moments for the purpose of prayer and intercession that bring My will to pass and My Kingdom into the earth in greater measure. I am calling you to incline your ear to Me, to seek first My Kingdom, and to receive My angels of revelation.

I have embraced the messages from angels of revelation, which is part of the fruit of this book. I believe the war room is one of the secret rooms in heaven. Since this prophetic encounter in the war room I am about to share in the next chapter, I have seen other rooms in the Father's house. But this vision of the war room was more vivid and lasted longer than anything I've seen before as of 2019. What I am about to share is an epic vision, a vision that extends beyond the normal length and detail of a general vision. Epic visions have a story line with tremendous detail and often plenty of drama.

It's often difficult to fully describe in human terms what you see in the spirit realm. Ezekiel did his best to describe the wheel within the wheel and the four living creatures. John did his best to chronicle what he saw in the Book of Revelation. Sometimes there are just no human words to articulate prophetic encounters. With that said, I will do my best.

With regard to revelation, it was 12th century mystic Hildegard of Bingen who said, "A fiery light, flashing intensely, came from the open vault of heaven and poured through my whole brain. Like a flame that is hot without burning it kindled all my heart and all my breast...Suddenly I could understand."[6] Her best known work is *Scito vias Domini*, which contains 26 visions where she speaks prophetically about knowing the ways of the Lord.

"I spoke and wrote these things not by the invention of my heart or that of any other person," she said, "but as by the secret mysteries of God; I heard and received them in the heavenly places. And again I heard a voice from heaven saying to me, 'Cry out therefore, and write thus!'" It is in that spirit that I write this vision and the pages that follow.

NOTES

1. Rev. Thomas Smith, ed., *Letters of the Rev. Samuel Rutherford* (Edinburgh and London: Oliphant, Edison, and Ferrier, 1891), 311.

2. James Burton Coffman, "Commentary on John 14:2," in *Coffman Commentaries on the Old and New Testament* (Abilene, Texas: Abilene Christian University Press, 1983-1999), https://www.studylight.org/commentaries/bcc/john-14.html.

3. John Paul Jackson, "Engaging the Revelatory Realm Part 2," TBN, If We Will Humble Ourselves, He Will Give Us More, March 22, 2004, http://injesus.com/messages/content/236886.

4. Miguel de Molinos, "Three Kinds of Silence," qtd. in Gene Edwards, *100 Days in the Secret Place* (Shippensburg, PA: Destiny Image Publishers, 2016), 116.

5. Jennifer LeClaire, *Mornings with the Holy Spirit* (Lake Mary, FL: Charisma House, 2015), 178.

6. Christianity Today, "Hildegard of Bingen," https://www.christianitytoday.com/history/people/innertravelers/hildegard-of-bingen.html.

CHAPTER 4

I SAW THE

WAR ROOM IN HEAVEN

In the vision, I saw a room in heaven. I can best describe as something like the Situation Room in the White House. It was a war room where strategies and tactics for spiritual battles were outlined for the angels and the elect who would be sent into the skirmish to execute God's will on the earth. While I could not see the Godhead in clear view, I felt the presence of Father God, Jesus, and the Holy Spirit. I saw the Father's arms at the head of the table. His fingers were crossed as He held His hands together.

Sitting at the table in designated seats were angels and saints. I saw warriors from the pages of the Bible in plain view. David, the worshiping warrior, was an active participant. Joshua and Gideon had a seat at the table. Warring angels whose name I don't know were sitting erect with their ears perked up, waiting for their next assignment. The glory surrounding God left a mist in the room that was almost tangible.

I could not hear every word spoken, but I discerned the intensity of this strategic meeting. The finger of God was pointing to different places on a world map. As He would point to specific nations and cities, those areas of the map would light up with fire and glory. These are hotbeds of spiritual activity in the earth—areas where there is a battle for transforming revival that precedes what is perhaps the final harvest.

I saw the Godhead communing together. They were in joyful agreement. I saw the pleasure of the Lord in preparing an army for this battle because He sees the victory and He laughs at His enemies. The great cloud of warrior witnesses was watching and the angels were listening with great intent in this war room. There was anticipation in the air.

Suddenly, the Father started handing out war assignments to the angels present at the table. These were princes that would lead heavenly hosts in an epic battle. These massive warring angels were standing at attention waiting with their heads and muscular chests held high. Father was dispatching them with specific assignments on the earth. He sent one to fight death, one to fight disease, and one to fight Jezebel. I did not see or hear all the assignments.

PEERING INTO THE WEAPONS CHEST

Next, I saw a weaponry chest open before my eyes. It contained many weapons, but swords sharpened for this specific battle drew my attention. I also saw oil, representing the anointing, poured out on the weapons. What did these sharpened, newly anointed swords represent? New revelation from the Word of God that would help soldiers on earth battle enemies in the second heaven.

Sharper swords were being handed out to those who were called to fight in this new warfare. The Holy Spirit is pouring out new revelations of warfare strategies—wisdom for the warfare. This wisdom is hidden in mysteries in the written Word of God. The wisdom for the warfare has always been in the Word, but these mysteries are being unlocked for the elect in this hour. Holy Spirit is going to lead and guide Christ's earthly army into the truth about tricky situations and difficult battles—truth that will lead to swifter victories than in generations past. Holy Spirit is going to give the elect a clear battle plan and a battle strategy.

I heard the Lord say, "We need to assign new generals of war in this season because some have gone on to glory." I saw Jesus anointing and commissioning generals, captains, sergeants. Jesus put His sword on the right shoulder of each officer in a commissioning ceremony. These generals were assigned to rally together captains and corporals and sergeants to wage warfare under the command of the Lord Jesus Christ.

COMMISSIONING NEW GENERALS

As Jesus was commissioning these generals of war, I saw angels standing right behind each one He was commissioning. It looked almost like catchers in a church who stand behind those who are receiving the laying on of hands in response to an altar call. However, I believe these were warring angels assigned to the generals to help them in battle. The angel's shadow almost seemed to clothe them and fell in front of them. That's how closely the warring angels assigned to these generals will walk with them.

Clearly, the Lord is growing ever more serious about the spiritual war we're in, and He's looking for those who will rise up and fight the darkness that's encroaching on the world and the church in the end times.

Fast-forwarding into the future—at what point this will happen I do not know—I see a vast army rising in a triangular formation with a newly minted general and his/her angel leading the charge. I see ranks spreading out line by line behind these commanders, a prophetic people who hear the Lord so freely they are able to turn on a dime. I see a trust forming between generals and the ranks so soldiers stop breaking ranks claiming "the Holy Spirit told me."

I see an authentic trust, a unity so strong that when one hears orders from heaven, the others are hearing the same thing. There's no question as to what to do because everybody is hearing the same voice.

This new level of warfare requires companies of warriors who understand order and authority. I see a new-breed army receiving warfare strategies straight from the war room in heaven like David, Gideon, and Joshua did. While many spiritual warriors have conquered based on experience from past wars, heaven's war room revelation will be vital to winning end-times battles. Man's strategies won't always win the battle. Heaven's blueprints will never lead to loss.

UNITY COMMANDS VICTORY

I saw mountains. I saw vast armies of prayer warriors establishing a presence at the base of the mountain and from strategic places on the mountain before invading the mountain and establishing beachheads.

Strategic intercession empowered the invasion. In the vision, I saw small units of prayer warriors moving in lockstep together into the mountains on reconnaissance missions like the 12 spies whom Moses sent to spy out the Promised Land.

Every believer has a part to play—but not all are generals. In this assignment, it's critical that everyone is in their exact ordained position, understanding that as the body has many parts so does the army of God. Can the eye say to the ear, "I don't have need of you"? Or the foot to the hand, "I have no need of you"? Some will be promoted rank by rank and some will progress in revelation little by little as they can handle it.

I saw what looked like Jacob's Ladder with angels ascending and descending. Some of those angels are carrying immediate revelation in the form of messages to the soldiers on the front lines and some are coming from heaven to back up soldiers on the ground.

Now is the time to see the seriousness of the hour and discern the times. It's time to stop playing church. It's time to stop allowing offense to come in between members of the Body like a cancer that rots the bones. It's time to stop pushing our way into places we don't belong because it's harmful.

I see offense as this major weapon in the end-times battle for souls. The Bible says, "No weapon formed against you shall prosper" (Isa. 54:17) in the context of the enemy forming weapons against us. This is absolute truth. Unfortunately, many in the Body of Christ are forming this weapon of offense and releasing it into the Body, causing many to stumble. The spirit of offense that's running rampant in the church is causing much carnage in the Body. I liken it to an autoimmune disease. We've turned against ourselves. We are battling each other.

Prophetically speaking, once we stop battling each other and turn our mouths and our minds and our hearts toward defeating a common enemy, the strategies He's given us will actually work—and we will be able to sustain the victory.

In times past, He has poured out strategies for warfare but they were ineffective because we didn't execute them due to offense that led to friendly fire. We stopped short of fulfilling the strategy because of personal pain, because of corporate pain, because someone broke rank and released friendly fire or pulled in the opposite direction out of rebellion or pride. A house divided cannot stand, and that's what the enemy is counting on. But we will stand. Jesus is coming back for a church without spot or wrinkle (see Eph. 5:26-27). I do not know when He is coming back, but I believe it's sooner than many think.

CHAPTER 5

THE MYSTERY
OF THE WAR IN HEAVEN

One day there was a war in heaven. Yes, war broke out in heaven. Revelation 12 gives us a quick glimpse into this short-lived war—short-lived because a prideful principality has no chance against the Prince of Peace. Revelation 12:7-9 reads:

> *And war broke out in heaven: Michael and his angels fought with the dragon; and the dragon and his angels fought, but they did not prevail, nor was a place found for them in heaven any longer. So the great dragon was cast out, that serpent of old, called the Devil and Satan, who deceives the whole world; he was cast to the earth, and his angels were cast out with him.*

The war in heaven is itself somewhat of a mystery. Here's what we know. The war was between the devil and Michael the archangel. In Luke 10:19, Jesus said He saw satan fall from heaven as lightning. This was the insurrection in which two-thirds of the angels were cast to the earth. We see little in the Bible about satan's fall, but there are a few references that cast more light on the sin leading up to this epic event. Ezekiel 28:16-17 reveals:

> *By the multitude of your merchandise, you were filled with violence in your midst, and you sinned; therefore I have cast you as profane out of the mountain of God; and I have destroyed you, O covering cherub, from the midst of the stones of fire. Your heart was lifted up because of your beauty; you have corrupted your wisdom by reason of your brightness; I cast you to the ground, I lay you before kings, that they may see you* (MEV).

The name lucifer is actually only used once time in the Bible in Isaiah 14:12-15, where we get more insight into his fall:

> *How are you fallen from heaven, O Lucifer, son of the morning! How you are cut down to the ground, you who weaken the nations! For you have said in your heart, "I will ascend into heaven, I will exalt my throne above the stars of God; I will sit also on the mount of the congregation, in the recesses of the north; I will ascend above the heights of the clouds, I will be like the Most High." Yet you shall be brought down to Hell, to the sides of the pit* (MEV).

SEEING THE WAR IN HEAVEN

But what happened in the war? Again, it's a mystery. I have prayed, and prayed, and read countless commentaries on this topic, which have various views. Some say Michael represents mankind. Others say he's a type of Christ. Ultimately, this is a picture of satan making war against the church. One day, we may have more revelation on the mystery, but of this I am confident: When the war broke out in heaven, God developed a strategy to cast him out.

Barnes' Notes on the Bible reads, "If Satan is permitted to make war against the church, there is no improbability in supposing that, in those higher regions where the war is carried on, and in those aspects of it which lie beyond the power and the knowledge of man, good angels should be employed to defeat his plans."

We know God dispatched Michael and other warring angels to fight lucifer and the angels who agreed with his betrayal. God did not do so without forethought. He developed a strategic battle plan, organized the heavenly hosts, and commissioned them to war. I imagine He did this from the war room in heaven. This is what I saw—and others have seen it also.

SEEING HEAVEN'S SITUATION ROOM

When I saw the war room in heaven, the best way I could describe it was like unto the Situation Room in the White House. What we call the Situation Room is a conference room and intelligence management center in the basement of the West Wing of the White House.

Security officials such as the National Security Advisor, the Homeland Security Advisor, and the White House Chief of Staff monitor and deal with domestic and foreign crises. There you'll find secure, advanced communication equipment so the President can maintain command and control of United States armed forces wherever they are sent.

Around the clock—24 hours a day and 365 days a year—Watch Teams monitor what is going on in the United States and abroad. Communications specialists and intelligence analysts are part of the staff. In the Situation Room, highly classified information is shared. Ingoing and outgoing information is encrypted.

This is the type of activity I saw in the war room. One wall of the war room—which appears like a command center—has images from both heaven and earth showing real-time events, according to what Dr. Linda Smith, co-founder of Free Them Ministries, says she saw in the spirit. These images, she explains, also had the supernatural ability to impart history as it relates to real-time events:

> The only thing that matters in these images is what is happening in the spirit realm. Although people, leaders are making decisions and engaging in activities, as one gazes on the images, one discerns the spiritual activity behind temporal events.
>
> In this same section is a large table like a conference table. Jesus is there, I am there and there are amazing creatures, angels I think, that are obviously assigned to military-like responsibilities. They are completely serious. There is no room for frivolity in this room.[1]

Smith describes the angels in the war room as about seven feet tall, broad shouldered, and strong in might and determination. These angels, she says, had steel feathers with very sharp edges, leather, chain mail, swords at their sides—and the whole armor of God.

The angels, Jesus, and I lean over this table, which has a small open square in the center, which looks at the earth through space through which we can view angelic, spirit activity as "they" carry out their assignments. We can also see the effect on the enemy, the evil spirits.[2]

CLOUD OF WITNESSES IN THE WAR ROOM

When I saw the war room in heaven, I saw part of the great cloud of witnesses. Hebrews 12:1 says, "Wherefore seeing we also are compassed about with so great a cloud of witnesses, let us lay aside every weight, and the sin which doth so easily beset us, and let us run with patience the race that is set before us" (KJV).

Some commentators believe the cloud of witnesses is the multitude of those who have died in the faith. Others say it's those in the Hebrews 11 Hall of Faith, including Abraham, Isaac, Jacob, Moses, Gideon, David, and the prophets who, of course, would be included in that multitude. In my war room vision, I saw Joshua, who is inferred in Hebrews 11, Gideon, and David.

Marty Breeden, founder of VictoryEmbraced Ministries, reports he had what he calls a "very vivid dream" of what looked like a war room in heaven.[3] He recognized what some would subscribe as part of the great cloud of witnesses mentioned in Hebrews 12:1 that surround us. Specifically, Breeden says he saw David Wilkerson, Leonard Ravenhill, Keith Green, and many others. He says he didn't recognize all of them.

They appeared to be continuing to go over strategic plans as to what information to release to the prophets of God next...to warn the people of God of that which is coming! I remember distinctly hearing one of them say as they viewed events upon the Earth and things that they said while in Ministry upon the Earth: "Yes, we covered that!" "Yes, we warned them about that!" "Yes, we told them about that!"

It was then that I saw two powerful men of God looking at one another, being *very serious* and saying: "Then they *have* to know by now that this thing is wrapping up right?" I then heard a voice from behind me, unseen, but I *knew that voice*. He said: "Yes, in their hearts they *know*, for they have been told...and those that *were* told, also *have told*. They know!"[4]

WEAPONS ON THE WALLS

Brynn Shamp offers a different perspective on the war room in heaven. In her vision, she says she saw the war room with a large mahogany table filling the majority of the room. High black chairs surrounded the table. She described intricate woodwork that stretched halfway up the walls.

Weapons were hanging in these cabinet-like sections along the walls. There hung a long thin sword to the left and Jesus took it down and handed it to me. As he gave it to me I heard, "Arise to the brightness of his shining"… which I understood as, Isaiah 60:1, "Arise, shine; for thy light is come, and the glory of the Lord is risen upon thee." I glanced up and there on the adjacent wall was a crossbow hanging and a men's suit of armor. I heard, "It is the Sword of the Lord and the Cross of Christ!"[5]

We'll talk more about the sword of the Lord in another chapter. No one else in visions of the war room I've read has seen arrows, but I know there are arrows in the war room. The enemy launches fiery darts. The enemy only counterfeits God's weaponry. I heard the Lord say:

Demonic fiery darts are no match for divine arrows from heaven. For I have given you the shield to quench every single flaming missile the enemy throws your way. But I have also given you divine arrows of deliverance to shoot at the heart of the enemy's plans to put you and keep you in bondage. I have given you strength to bend a bow of bronze. Remember, the battle is ultimately Mine and I will use My own arrows against the onslaught if I need to. Trust in Me.

WAR ROOM ATMOSPHERE

My friend Ana Werner shares her visitation to a war room in heaven in her book *Seeing Behind the Veil*. She describes the atmosphere as exciting and the energy was high. When she walked into the war room, the first thing she noticed was Jesus at the center.

> Angels bustled to and fro in the room; they were huge and majestic. Some wore armor and carried weapons. I was taken aback a little by their size and magnitude. They were dressed and ready to go into a war. Some of them blew horns at specific times while I was in this room, and they pointed the horn in a specific direction as they released its sound. I was sure they were releasing the presence of the King over a certain region of the world. The sound of horns would release breakthrough. No matter what the angels did, though, they kept their eyes on the King in the center of the room. They were taking their cues from Him.[6]

Werner says she was also drawn to and intrigued by the number of people in the room. She saw them dressed in white robes in a peaceful state. Although they carried peace, she says, they were not there to make peace but war. She heard loud prayers, intercession, and declarations in the war room—like a war cry. She says it sounded like thunder shattering the air.

SEEING THE WORLD OUTSIDE THE WINDOWS

Simon Braker, a member of the core leadership team of the British Isles Council of Prophets and co-founder of Legacy Ministries

International, says he saw what would best be described as a war room like you would see in a Second World War movie, but it was massive. He describes his vision:

> There was a large long table that would sit a massive number. The room had glass windows all around and I could see the world out the windows like we were above the earth. The room was filled with generals each one had a roll of paper like a blueprint, each one came in and they unrolled their plan and they all then became excited as they began to share their plan.
>
> I could hear words like, "strategy," "growth" and "mobilisation" being used. The whole feeling of the room was very excited. Suddenly the room went silent as the door opened and a man walked in. Immediately I knew it was Jesus. He walked to the top of the table and sat down. It was quiet for a few moments, then he spoke and said, "Friends have you brought your plans?" People began to speak excitedly and shared as they showed their blueprint on the table.
>
> Jesus just sat and waited as each one spoke. It went quiet again, then Jesus stood up and flung a cloth across the length of the table. It rolled out like the train of a robe; it covered all the other plans. Again it was quiet for a moment, then wine began to pour out of the table top. Everyone was shocked by the speed. It literally began to flood the room at speed.
>
> This was a big space where hundreds sat around the table. In seconds the room was knee deep and very quickly the

room was full. Then all of the glass windows shattered and the wine began to pour out the windows upon the earth. I saw the Lord. He was laughing. Jesus said, "We have seen what you can do, know and watch what I can do." The force of the flow was such that everyone in the room were being flung about. It was holy wonderful chaos.[7]

In the next chapter, we will explore the mystery of Jehovah's war room.

NOTES

1. Dr. Linda Smith, "War Room in Heaven," XP Media, 2013, https://www.xpmedia.com/article/12854/war-room-in-heaven.

2. Ibid.

3. Marty Breeden, "Dream: War Room in Heaven," 444 Prophecy News, June 13, 2018, https://444prophecynews.com/dream -war-room-in-heaven-marty-breeden.

4. Ibid.

5. Brynn Shamp, "A Prophetic Vision of the War Room of Heaven," Awakening Magazine, June 17, 2016 https://awakeningmag .com/a-prophetic-vision-of-the-war-room-of-heaven.

6. Ana Werner, *Seeing Behind the Veil* (Shippensburg, PA: Destiny Image Publishers, 2018), 59-60.

7. Simon Braker, "UK Prophet Has War Room Vision With Covid-19," 365 Prophetic, April 28, 2020, https://365prophetic .com/hi/2020/04/28/uk-prophet-has-war-room-vision-with -covid-19.

CHAPTER 6

THE MYSTERY
OF JEHOVAH'S WAR ROOM

Angels and saints were sitting at a colossal boardroom table in a cloudy room unconfined by space or time. Enveloped in a tangible glory, the atmosphere was charged with life and pregnant with victory, but the tone in the room was resolute. At the head of the table in a high-backed chair sat Father God, Jehovah Gibbor. He held one of His hands in the other, with fingers crossed. His posture was not just confident but communicated His omnipotence. Words cannot describe.

I could not see His face, but I saw His hands—I saw the hands that made all things. I saw the fingers that ordained the moon and the stars. I saw the mighty hand that delivered the Israelites from the Egyptian army. I saw the hands that spread out the heavens. The hands that mold us on the potter's wheel into the image of Christ. I saw the hands that hold the depths of the earth and the peaks of the mountains.

I could not see His feet, but I saw His hands. I saw the hands that pierced the fleeing serpent. I saw the hands that hold our times. I saw the hands that open to give us blessings. I saw the hand that holds power and might. I saw the hand that does valiantly for His people. I saw the hand that stretches out against His enemies to destroy them. I saw the hand that saves.

I could not see His frame, but I saw His hands. I saw the hands that act for the sake of His name. I saw the hands that uphold us and establish us. I saw the hands that lead us and guide us. I saw the hands that formed mankind into His image. The mere sight of His hands was awesome and terrifying, covered with lightning with rays flashing forth. I saw His hands. I was mesmerized by the sight of His hands.

After meditating on the glory of His hands, I saw seats designated for heaven's elite. I saw warriors like Joshua, judges like Gideon, and kings like David. Michael the archangel was there, along with other high-ranking warring angels whose names I do not know. The angels were sitting erect—at attention—with their ears perked up, waiting for their next assignment. As Scripture describes in Psalm 103, these angels were actively listening to the voice of God's Word to execute His will on the earth.

I saw the war room in heaven. There was perfect peace with no hint of confusion, strife, or any evil work. It was the place our God of War assembles His angels to plan for battle in the second heaven.

HEAVEN'S SITUATION ROOM

Words don't do this description justice, but God's War Room looked something like the Situation Room in the White House.

Strategies and tactics for spiritual battles were outlined for the angels and elect who would be sent into the satanic skirmish to execute God's will on the earth. The spirit of prayer was in the room, crying, "Thy will be done, on earth as it is in heaven."

At times, I could not hear the words the Father, Son, and Holy Spirit shared. I could only see lips moving because of the thick glory manifesting. I sensed the information revealed was not for human ears to hear. This highly classified information was sealed from my hearing. That did not dampen what I discerned. The intensity of the meeting was a Code Red.

The finger of God was pointing to various places on a world map—the finger of God pointing to the earth He created as the battle between darkness and light comes to a head.

As Creator God pointed to specific nations and cities, those areas of the map would light up with fire and glory that overcame encroaching darkness. Creator God is releasing spiritual awakening in strategic areas where the battle for transforming revival is raging. I sensed God was preparing for the final harvest, or at least the harvest of harvesters for the final harvest.

SEEING PSALM 2 REALITIES

The Godhead was communing together in joyful agreement. I immediately recalled Psalm 2:1-6:

Why are the nations so angry? Why do they waste their time with futile plans? The kings of the earth prepare for battle; the rulers plot together against the Lord and against his anointed one. "Let us break their chains," they cry, "and free ourselves from slavery to God." But the one who rules in heaven laughs. The Lord scoffs at them. Then in anger he rebukes them, terrifying them with his fierce fury. For the Lord declares, "I have placed my chosen king on the throne in Jerusalem, on my holy mountain" (NLT).

Again, I felt the pleasure of the Lord in preparing an army for this battle because He sees the victory and He laughs at His enemies. The great cloud of witnesses was looking into the Master's master plan. Angels were listening with great intent in this war room. The anticipation in the room almost took my breath away, but what happened struck me with awe.

The Father started handing out war assignments to the angels present at the table. As I mentioned, these angels were princes working for the Kingdom of light that would lead heavenly hosts in an epic battle. These massive warring angels were standing at attention waiting with their heads and chests held high. Jesus was dispatching them with specific assignments on the earth. Again, He sent one to fight death, one to fight disease, and one of fight Jezebel. I did not see or hear all the assignments.

A DEEPER LOOK AT GOD'S WEAPONRY

A weaponry chest opened before my eyes. Inside I saw many weapons, but swords sharpened for this specific battle demanded my attention. Newly sharpened, newly anointed swords represent new revelation from the Word of God that would help soldiers on earth battle enemies in the second heaven. The weapons of His warfare are not carnal, but mighty to pull down enemy strongholds (see 2 Cor. 10:4).

Suddenly, I understood more fully Isaiah 54:17: no weapon formed against us will prosper. Suddenly, I got a greater revelation that we are God's war club (see Jer. 51:20). Suddenly, I recalled not only the mighty exploits of David but also the exploits of David's mighty men who slew hundreds individually as the spirit of might rested upon them. Suddenly, I understood in this epic battle we are armed with every kind of weapon of war—but more than that, we have wisdom to know what weapon to wield and when to wield it.

In the war chest were the Lord's weapons of war. The chest was overflowing with weapons deadly to the enemy's camp. There were weapons of fire that would burn up the enemy's weapons. Lethal weapons. Weapons of righteousness that defy weapons of wickedness. Some of the weapons were words of decree, prophetic words, and words of praise and worship.

The Holy Spirit is going to lead and guide Christ's earthly army into the truth about the root of enemy onslaughts, demonic snares, and satanic battles—truth that will lead to swifter victories than in generations past. Holy Spirit is going to give the elect a clear battle plan and a battle strategy that will not fail. God always leads us into triumph in Christ (see 2 Cor. 2:14).

SECRET, CLOSED-DOOR COMMISSIONINGS

I heard the Lord say, "We need to assign new generals of war in this season because some have gone on to glory." Jesus was anointing and commissioning generals, captains, and sergeants with a Davidic anointing. David, the worshiping warrior, never lost a battle. Jesus put His sword on the right shoulder of each officer in an elaborate commissioning ceremony only visible in the war room.

God is going to begin to encounter believers in private commissioning ceremonies of which they are not to speak. (And they will not be posted on social media.) I am reminded of Jehu's commissioning. Jehu was not anointed to be king in front of his brothers. God told Elisha to make sure Jehu was commissioned in an inner room (see 2 Kings 9:2). Jehu went on to decimate the house of Ahab and Jezebel, and no one expected the onslaught.

Likewise, no one will know who was enlisted into these special forces—no one but those commissioned and the population of the war room who is present at the secret ceremony. Secrecy is important as satan will go after new-breed generals with fierce anger. Of course, these generals will become evident as the war rages hotter, but no earthy fanfare will tip the hand of God. The demonic agents will be blindsided with divine suddenlies.

As Jesus was commissioning these generals of war, angels stood behind each one. It looked something like catchers in a church who stand behind those who are receiving the laying on of hands in response to an altar call. However, I believe these warring angels were not standing there as heavenly catchers. They were assigned to the generals to help them in battle. The angels' shadows, which were cast over and in front of the generals, seemed to clothe them with protection. That's how closely the warring angels assigned to these generals, assigned to rally the Body to wage warfare under the command of the Lord Jesus Christ, will walk with them.

A TRIANGULAR FORMATION

Fast-forward into the future—I do not know the day or time—I see what looks like an ocean of Christian army troops advancing in triangular formation with a newly minted general and his (or her) angel leading the charge. Angels and saints are working together under the rulership of the Captain of the Hosts, the Head of the Church, Jesus Christ. Angel armies accompany earth's armies into a blockbuster battle of heavenly proportions.

I see soldiers of all ranks spreading out line by line behind these commanders. From my perspective, it looks like wave after wave in a rhythmic high tide. When the waves crash against the shoreline, the enemy retreats. You could compare it to a battering ram that keeps punishing its opponent. The opponents include principalities, powers, rulers of the darkness and spiritual wickedness in high places.

I see a trust forming between generals and the soldiers so no one claims "the Holy Spirit told me something different" and takes on a heart posture that births strife in the heat of the battle. Internal attacks will come. Though some will fall away, becoming lovers of self and refusing to submit to authority, a remnant of the unified will overcome hordes of hell.

Within the remnant, I see an authentic trust, a unity so strong that when generals hear marching orders from heaven, the ranks are hearing the same voice at the same time. There will be enemy interference, but the enemy's voice has no sway on the chosen, who will cast down imaginations and every high thing exalted against the knowledge of God (see 2 Cor. 10:5).

This new level of warfare demands companies of warriors that are teachable. This new-breed army will receive warfare strategies straight from the war room in heaven—like David, Gideon, and Joshua did—to fight enemies they never even knew existed. While many spiritual warriors have conquered based on experience from past wars, heaven's war room revelation will be vital to winning end-times battles. While man's strategies won't always win the battle, heaven's blueprints will never lead to loss.

I SEE THE REMNANT RISING

Prophetically speaking, I see the remnant rising. The remnant is the church within the church. The remnant is a small number of people among a large crowd. It's a group of survivors with boldness to do and say what the Lord wants done and said despite the personal cost. God is activating the remnant in a new way in this hour. I heard the Lord say:

> *I am calling forth My remnant, those who will cooperate with My Spirit and with truth; those who will speak forth the words that I put in their mouth no matter who*

likes it and no matter who doesn't like it. For I have called you to gather together and to band together in small groups and even large groups. But unified groups are what I am after. I am after groups of unified believers who are crying out in My name so I can hear their voice and heal their land.

Who will gather? Who will be part of the remnant that I am calling together in this hour? The praying church, the on-fire believers, the ones who will not take no for an answer when the enemy is standing in the way between what I've called you to and the reality of the promise.

I am rising. I am rising. My Spirit is rising and I am looking for the remnant to rise with Me. Who will ascend to the holy hill, to the mountain of the Most High? Those with clean hands and a pure heart. The remnant. I am calling the remnant. I am calling the remnant. I am calling the remnant.

I am calling you out of your caves and out of your closets. I'm calling some of you out of your churches. I'm calling some of you out of the business world and into ministry. I am calling the remnant. I am calling the remnant to prayer. I want to hear the prayers of the remnant, unified, unified, unified, unified, unified, unified together, touching and agreeing together.

CHAPTER 7

THE MYSTERY

OF JEHOVAH GIBBOR MILCHAMAH

Jehovah Gibbor was the leading character in the war room. Many people know God as Jehovah Nissi, our banner. Many know Him as Jehovah Jireh, our provider. Many know Him as Jehovah Rapha, our healer. But in this vision our heavenly Father was manifesting as *Jehovah Gibbor Milchamah*, the Lord mighty in battle. But Jehovah Gibbor is yet a mystery to many believers. It's time to unravel this mystery in the new era of the church.

Indeed, many believers have never even heard Father referred to as Jehovah Gibbor Milchamah, but we find this in the pages of Scripture. Psalm 24:8 reveals: "Who is this King of glory? The Lord strong and mighty, the Lord mighty in battle." Job declared, "He runs at me like a warrior" (Job 16:14). And Exodus 15:3 assures, "The Lord is a man of war; the Lord is His name."

Zephaniah 3:17 declares, "The Lord your God is in your midst, a victorious warrior" (NASB). And Isaiah 42:13 assures us: "The

Lord shall go forth like a mighty man; He shall stir up His zeal like a man of war. He shall cry out, yes, shout aloud; He shall prevail against His enemies." Indeed, Jehovah Gibbor knows how to fight—and win. He's never lost a battle—and He's a master battle planner.

Driver and Briggs's Hebrew and English Lexicon of the Old Testament translates El Gibbor as "mighty hero or divine hero, reflecting the divine majesty." Other translators say it means "powerful champion." All of these define the Lord Jesus Christ, the captain of the hosts whom Joshua encountered before heading out to battle.

Remember, our God—Jehovah Gibbor—was outlining a strategy for an epic battle in His war room. As you'll recall, the Godhead was communing together, and I saw the pleasure of the Lord in preparing an army for this battle because He sees the victory and He laughs at His enemies.

JEHOVAH GIBBOR: OUR MASTER BATTLE STRATEGIST

In Isaiah 9:6, we see the Lord as an "extraordinary strategist" (TPT), a term referring to His role as King, and a king's ability to devise military strategy. Just as Jehovah Gibbor had a strategy to create the heavens and the earth and everything in it, He has strategies for overwhelming victory in every war. Jehovah Gibbor sees the end from the beginning—and He declares the end from the beginning (see Isa. 46:10). In fact, He is the end and the beginning—the Alpha and Omega. If the fight is fixed, the war is won.

With the epic vision of the war room in mind, it's important to understand Jehovah Gibbor as omniscient, omnipotent, and omnipresent. Jehovah Gibbor is omniscient—He knows everything. Jehovah Gibbor doesn't have to wonder what the enemy is going to do next—He already knows. And Jehovah Gibbor can tell you or show you what the enemy of your soul will do next. When Jeremiah's enemies threatened his life, he was able to prepare. Jeremiah said, "Now the Lord gave me knowledge of it, and I know it; for You showed me their doings" (Jer. 11:18).

Similarly, we see an account in Second Kings 6:8-12 that demonstrates how Jehovah Gibbor will show us the enemy's strategy so we can combat it:

> *Now the king of Syria was making war against Israel; and he consulted with his servants, saying, "My camp will be in such and such a place." And the man of God sent to the king of Israel, saying, "Beware that you do not pass this place, for the Syrians are coming down there." Then the king of Israel sent someone to the place of which the man of God had told him. Thus he warned him, and he was watchful there, not just once or twice.*
>
> *Therefore the heart of the king of Syria was greatly troubled by this thing; and he called his servants and said to them, "Will you not show me which of us is for the king of Israel?" And one of his servants said, "None, my lord, O king; but Elisha, the prophet who is in Israel, tells the king of Israel the words that you speak in your bedroom."*

Imagine how frustrating it is for the enemy to know that you know his next move before we make it. If we will draw close to Jehovah Gibbor, He will show us things to come in battle so that we can dodge the devil's fiery darts. We can ambush the enemy who's trying to ambush us. We can frustrate his plans at every turn.

Jehovah Gibbor is also omnipotent—He is all powerful. Christ shared His power with us to overcome the wicked one. He has given us authority over all the power of the enemy (see Luke 10:19). We need a revelation of Jehovah Gibbor's exceeding great power available to us as believers (see Eph. 1:19). We need to grasp the reality that the power that raised Christ from the dead dwells in us and Jesus is seated far above every enemy (see Eph. 1:21). Jehovah Gibbor is omnipresent—He is present everywhere all the time. Jehovah Gibbor our refuge and our strength, a very present help in time of war (see Ps. 46:1).

JEHOVAH GIBBOR SHARES HIS PLANS

Jehovah Gibbor has a detailed battle plan for every fight we face. This is a promise in Second Corinthians 2:14: "Now thanks be to God who always leads us in triumph in Christ, and through us diffuses the fragrance of His knowledge in every place." Proverbs 24:6 tells us, "Strategic planning is the key to warfare; to win, you need a lot of good counsel" (MSG). There's no better counsel than Jehovah Gibbor's counsel.

In order to see the victory Jehovah Gibbor has planned for us in every war, we must follow His leadership on the battlefield. We must also understand His spiritual warfare strategy for today's battle may be vastly different than our warfare strategy for yesterday's battle—or future battles. Indeed, the Book of the Wars of the Lord mentioned in Numbers 21:14 is vast.

Consider Jehovah Gibbor's strategy for the Israelites in the Exodus 17 battle against the Amalekites. Moses charged Joshua with choosing men to go out and fight while he stood on top of the hill with God's rod in his hand. Sounds like a strange strategy, doesn't it? But it worked. Exodus 17:11-13 gives us the account:

> *And so it was, when Moses held up his hand, that Israel prevailed; and when he let down his hand, Amalek prevailed. But Moses' hands became heavy; so they took a stone and put it under him, and he sat on it. And Aaron and Hur supported his hands, one on one side, and the other on the other side; and his hands were steady until the going down of the sun. So Joshua defeated Amalek and his people with the edge of the sword.*

JEHOVAH GIBBOR KEEPS THE ENEMY ON HIS HEELS

When Moses died and God mantled Joshua to take the Israelites into the Promised Land, Joshua didn't stand on a hill with God's rod. Jehovah Gibbor gave him a different strategy. You can read the full account in Joshua 6:2-17—and it had nothing to do with a rod.

Israel's men of war marched around Jericho once a day for six days. Seven priests with ram horn trumpets went with them. On the seventh day, they marched around Jericho seven times and the priests blew the trumpets, signaling the Israelites to shout as loud as they could. With that, Jehovah Gibbor promised, the walls would fall flat. And they did. From there, the Israelites rushed in and took the city.

When Joshua faced his next battle, though, the strategy was different. Jehovah Gibbor did not tell Joshua to march around the city of Ai day after day. Instead, after an initial defeat in battle, Jehovah Gibbor told Joshua to lay an ambush for the city behind it (see Josh. 8:2). In another battle, Joshua was moved to command the sun to stand still in battle (see Josh. 10). Clearly, we can't get too comfortable with what has worked in the past. Jehovah Gibbor does a new thing, even in the battlefield.

David also engaged in diverse warfare strategies from the Book of the Wars of the Lord. David defeated Goliath with a sling and a stone. David conquered Jerusalem by sending men into the impenetrable city by way of the water shaft (see 2 Sam. 5:8). David overcame Absalom's coup by planting spies on the inside of his son's camp. Once he depended on the sound of marching in the mulberry trees as God's green light to advance against the Philistine army (see 2 Sam. 5:24).

Time does not permit us to tap into the many warfare strategies Jehovah Gibbor gave His people against natural enemies. Jehovah Gibbor is still handing out fresh spiritual warfare strategies to believers today. Take some time to counsel in His war room before you set out to fight your next battle. Ask questions and wait for answers. The God of War will lead you into victory every time. Jehovah Maginnenu—the Lord Our Defense—will protect you in battle. Jehovah Magan—the Lord my Shield—will cover you as you advance.

DON'T BE IGNORANT OF THE DEVIL'S STRATEGY

Of course, the enemy is also strategic. We see the enemy exposed in Nahum 1:11 with strategy of his own: "From you, O Nineveh, one has marched forth who plots evil against the Lord, a wicked military strategist" (NET). In Second Corinthians 2:11, Paul warned us not to be ignorant of the devil's devices. Certainly, Jehovah Gibbor is not ignorant of the devil's devices, but sometimes we are. If we are going to cooperate with Jehovah Gibbor, we need to know our enemy.

> If you know the enemy and know yourself, you need not fear the result of a hundred battles. If you know yourself but not the enemy, for every victory gained you will also suffer a defeat. If you know neither the enemy nor yourself, you will succumb in every battle.

Those are the words of Sun Tzu, who wrote one of the most influential books on military strategy in history. Although we look to the Bible for our military strategy, knowing your enemy is certainly a biblical command. Paul tells us plainly in Second Corinthians 2:11 not to be ignorant of the devil's devices. The Greek word for *ignorant* in Seond Corinthians 2:11 is *agnoeo*, which in this context means "to be ignorant, not to know; not to understand, unknown," according to *The KJV New Testament Greek Lexicon*. We must be a student of God and His Word, but God warns about the enemy's nature, character, and ploys—and gives us clear examples of his machinations against the saints—throughout Scripture. Clearly, God does want us to understand the enemy's devices. Some translations say "sly ways," "schemes," "designs," "intentions," and "thoughts."

The word *devices* in Second Corinthians 2:11 comes from the Greek word *noema*, according to the lexicon. It means a material perception, "a mental perception, thought; an evil purpose; that which thinks, the mind, thoughts or purposes." Jehovah Gibbor is so good that in the very command not to be ignorant of the devil's devices He reveals what some of his devices are. The enemy works to skew our mental perceptions and thoughts. He has an evil purpose against our mind.

There is a war in your mind. There is a war in the heavens. There is a lot at stake. Know the enemy, know yourself, and know your God—Jehovah Gibbor. The war room in heaven is always open. The Isaiah 9:6 God—Jehovah Gibbor—always wins the battle. Jehovah Gibbor will come back with hair white like wool, with eyes like flames of fire, with feet like bronze, and a two-edged sword in His mouth. He will come again with the angel armies on His side.

I heard Jehovah Gibbor say:

Just rest in the fact that breakthrough belongs to you. It is your portion. I already attained it for you. Just rest in that. Rest even in the warfare. Learn to rest while you fight. I will teach you. I will teach your hands to battle, and I will teach your fingers to war. I will teach you. I, Myself, will teach you. Learn of Me because I am meek and lowly of heart, but I am a warrior—the Captain of the host—and I am victorious always. That's My portion and that's My plan for you—never to lose a battle.

CHAPTER 8

THE MYSTERY
OF THE SWORD

Many spiritual warriors are fighting without a sword. They may strap on their helmet of salvation. They may remember to don their breastplate of righteousness. They may lace up their shoes of peace. They may tighten their belt of truth. They may even lift up the shield of faith. That's all good, but without the two-edged sword you can't slay the demons. We need to understand the mystery of the sword.

Remember, in the epic vision I saw a weaponry chest open before my eyes. It contained many weapons, but swords sharpened for this specific battle drew my attention. I also saw oil, representing the anointing, poured out on the weapons. I described some of what I saw earlier in the revelation. But I could not take my eyes off the sharpened, newly anointed swords representing new revelation.

Swords—whether stabbing swords or slashing swords—were used regularly in Bible times. In fact, the word *sword* is in the Bible 406 times. Some used slings and stones and others used spears. One man used an ox goad to kill six hundred Philistines (see Judg. 3:31), and Samson used the jawbone of a donkey to kill one thousand (see Judg. 15:16). But swords reigned supreme as a weapon of warfare—and still do in the spiritual wars we fight today.

It's not enough to have a sword. The sword must be sharp. You can strike a blow with a blunt sword, but you may not kill the enemy. Jehovah Chereb is saying, "Hammer your plowshares into swords and your pruning hooks into spears. Train even your weaklings to be warriors" (Joel 3:10 NLT).

SEEING THE LORD THE SWORD

Just as we need a revelation of Jehovah Gibbor in this season, we must also understand Jehovah Chereb, which translates "the Lord the Sword." We find this descriptor of our mighty God in Deuteronomy 33:29: "How blessed you are, O Israel! Who else is like you, a people saved by the Lord? He is your protecting shield and your triumphant sword! Your enemies will cringe before you, and you will stomp on their backs!" (NLT).

The Lord the Sword utterly destroys our enemies. Remember what King David, the worshiping warrior, once said—the battle belongs to the Lord (see 1 Sam. 17:47). And there are some battles that we do not have to fight. You could ask King Jehoshaphat and you can read the account in Second Chronicles when the Moabites, the Ammonites, and the others beside them determined to annihilate Israel during his rulership. Second Chronicles 20:15-17 leaves this account:

Thus says the Lord to you: "Do not be afraid nor dismayed because of this great multitude, for the battle is not yours, but God's. Tomorrow go down against them. They will surely come up by the Ascent of Ziz, and you will find them at the end of the brook before the Wilderness of Jeruel. You will not need to fight in this battle. Position yourselves, stand still and see the salvation of the Lord, who is with you."

Get to know the Lord the Sword and wait for His instruction. The battle is really His. Although we are His battle-axe, sometimes He intervenes Himself. Pray God will reveal the mystery of the sword.

SEEING THE SWORD OF THE LORD

Beyond the Lord the Sword is the sword of the Lord. The sword of the Lord represents the judgment of God on His enemies. Over and again, we see His people cry out for the sword of the Lord to fall.

In Psalm 17:13, David cries, "Arise, O Lord, confront him, cast him down; deliver my life from the wicked with Your sword." And again in Psalm 45:3, "Gird Your sword upon Your thigh, O Mighty One, with Your glory and Your majesty." The Lord Himself prophesies about His sword in Scripture. Let's look on these and meditate on them as we agree with Jehovah Chereb.

Isaiah 66:16 reads, "For by fire and by His sword the Lord will judge all flesh; and the slain of the Lord shall be many." Ezekiel 12:14 tells us, "I will scatter to every wind all who are around him to help him, and all his troops; and I will draw out the sword after them."

Leviticus 26:25 says, "And I will bring a sword against you that will execute the vengeance of the covenant; when you are gathered together within your cities I will send pestilence among you; and you shall be delivered into the hand of the enemy." Exodus 15:9 reads, "I will draw my sword, my hand shall destroy them." These are just a few very intense Scriptures. Here are a few more. Through Ezekiel, He said:

I will draw My sword out of its sheath and cut off from you the righteous and the wicked. Because I will cut off from you the righteous and the wicked, therefore My sword will go forth from its sheath against all flesh from south to north. Thus all flesh will know that I, the Lord, have drawn My sword out of its sheath. It will not return to its sheath again (Ezekiel 21:3-5 NASB).

In Isaiah 34:5-6, we read:

For My sword shall be bathed in heaven; Indeed, it shall come down on Edom, and on the people of My curse, for judgment. The sword of the Lord is filled with blood, it is made overflowing with fatness, with the blood of lambs and goats, with the fat of the kidneys of rams. For the Lord has a sacrifice in Bozrah, and a great slaughter in the land of Edom.

David understood this, saying: "If he does not turn back, He will sharpen His sword; He bends His bow and makes it ready" (Ps. 7:12). We need a revelation of the sword of the Lord and to listen in the midst of a heated battle for the Holy Spirit's leading to call for God to use it to judge His enemies who are plaguing us.

THE SWORD OF THE SPIRIT

You are surely familiar with the whole armor of God listed in Ephesians 6. Paul admonishes us to put on every piece so we can stand against the wiles of the devil. He goes on to mention a raging war with principalities, powers, rulers of the darkness, and spiritual wickedness in high places. Ephesians 6:14-20 informs:

> *Stand therefore, having girded your waist with truth, having put on the breastplate of righteousness, and having shod your feet with the preparation of the gospel of peace; above all, taking the shield of faith with which you will be able to quench all the fiery darts of the wicked one. And take the helmet of salvation, and the sword of the Spirit, which is the word of God; praying always with all prayer and supplication in the Spirit, being watchful to this end with all perseverance and supplication for all the saints—and for me, that utterance may be given to me, that I may open my mouth boldly to make known the mystery of the gospel, for which I am an ambassador in chains; that in it I may speak boldly, as I ought to speak.*

The sword of the Spirit is the Word of God. We wield it with our mouth. Isaiah said, "And He has made My mouth like a sharp sword" (Isa. 49:2). Speaking of Jesus, John the Revelator wrote: "Now out of His mouth goes a sharp sword, that with it He should strike the nations. And He Himself will rule them with a rod of iron. He Himself treads the winepress of the fierceness and wrath of Almighty God" (Rev. 19:15).

When you wield the sword with your mouth, you are releasing Hebrews 4:12 realities: "For the word of God is living and powerful, and sharper than any two-edged sword, piercing even to the division of soul and spirit, and of joints and marrow, and is a discerner of the thoughts and intents of the heart." I heard Jehovah Chereb say:

> *The days of warfare as usual are over. I am calling you to oil your shield and lift up your sword in a new way. The tactics that worked in the past will not work in the battles that are ahead. The new way is love. The new way is humility. Too many have taken pride in their spiritual warfare skills, which causes Me to resist them in the heat of the battle because apart from Me they can do nothing. War by walking in love. War by walking in My Word. Beyond this, I will show you new strategies for every individual skirmish. Lean on Me.*

WISDOM FOR THE WARFARE

During the epic vision of the war room in heaven, the Lord showed me wisdom is hidden in mysteries in the written Word of God. The wisdom for the warfare has always been in the Word, but these mysteries are being unlocked for the elect in this hour. Holy Spirit is going to lead and guide Jehovah Chereb's earthly army into the truth about tricky situations and difficult battles—truth that will lead to swifter victories than in generations past. Holy Spirit is going to give the elect a clear battle plan and a battle strategy.

I pray for many things every day. I pray for my family, my friends, my ministry, my nation—and, of course, myself. I pray for protection. I pray for a deeper revelation of God's love and over my life. I pray for grace. But there's one thing I've been praying for more and more lately—and I am convinced that if we would pray more for this one thing we would make better use of our time, live happier lives, and ultimately see more answers to our prayers.

What is this one thing I've been praying for more and more lately? Wisdom. I believe if we pray more for spiritual wisdom—even if it means praying less for natural needs—we'll receive more wisdom and our natural needs will be more than met. We could all take a hint from Solomon. You know the story. The Lord appealed to Solomon in a dream and made this invitation: "Ask! What shall I give you?" Can you imagine the Lord coming to you in a dream and making such an invitation? What would you ask God for if you could ask and assuredly receive anything?

It seems Solomon had enough wisdom to ask for the principal thing—wisdom. Solomon replied to God's invitation with these words: "Give to Your servant an understanding heart to judge Your people, that I may discern between good and evil. For who is able to judge this great people of Yours?" (1 Kings 3:9). That made God happy. Let's see how He responded in First Kings 3:11-14:

> *Because you have asked this thing, and have not asked long life for yourself, nor have asked riches for yourself, nor have asked the life of your enemies, but have asked for yourself*

understanding to discern justice, behold, I have done accord-
ing to your words; see, I have given you a wise and under-
standing heart, so that there has not been anyone like you
before you, nor shall any like you arise after you. And I
have also given you what you have not asked: both riches
and honor, so that there shall not be anyone like you among
the kings all your days. So if you walk in My ways, to keep
My statutes and My commandments, as your father David
walked, then I will lengthen your days.

All I can say to that is, "Wow and amen!"

WHAT WISDOM WILL DO FOR YOU

God is no respecter of persons (see Acts 10:34). You can receive the wisdom you need to walk according to God's battle plan for you. James clearly stated that "If any of you lacks wisdom, let him ask of God, who gives to all liberally and without reproach, and it will be given to him" (James 1:5). The only catch is you have to ask in faith, without doubting. That's not much of a catch, and it shouldn't be too hard to do. God wants to give you wisdom so you can walk wise, making the best use of your time because the days are evil (see Eph. 5:15-17). Let's check out what Solomon had to say in the wake of receiving such great wisdom:

Happy is the man who finds wisdom, and the man who gains
understanding; For her proceeds are better than the profits of
silver, and her gain than fine gold. She is more precious than

rubies, and all the things you may desire cannot compare with her. Length of days is in her right hand, in her left hand riches and honor. Her ways are ways of pleasantness, and all her paths are peace. She is a tree of life to those who take hold of her, and happy are all who retain her (Proverbs 3:13-18).

Wisdom begets wisdom. The ear of the wise seeks knowledge (see Prov. 18:15). The wise man listens to advice (see Prov. 12:15). A man's wisdom makes his face shine (see Eccles. 8:1). By wisdom your house is built (see Prov. 24:3). Wise ones are cautious and turn away from evil (see Prov. 14:16). The words of the wise win him favor (see Eccles. 10:12). The wise will inherit honor (see Prov. 3:35). Wisdom will keep and guard you if you love it (see Prov. 4:6-7). I could go on and on and encourage you to do a study of the benefits of walking in God's wisdom.

SEEKING WISDOM FOR WAR

When we receive wisdom, it's important that we acknowledge its source. The Lord gives wisdom (see Prov. 2:6). We should never be wise in our own eyes (see Prov. 3:7). But we should humbly pray for wisdom more and more. So these are my prayers. I pray like Solomon, who said, "Give to Your servant an understanding heart to judge Your people, that I may discern between good and evil" (1 Kings 3:9). And I pray like Paul, who asked:

That the God of our Lord Jesus Christ, the Father of glory, may give to you the spirit of wisdom and revelation in the knowledge of Him, the eyes of your understanding being enlightened; that you may know what is the hope of His calling, what are the riches of the glory of His inheritance in the saints, and what is the exceeding greatness of His power toward us who believe, according to the working of His mighty power which He worked in Christ when He raised Him from the dead and seated Him at His right hand in the heavenly places, far above all principality and power and might and dominion, and every name that is named, not only in this age but also in that which is to come (Ephesians 1:17-21).

And I pray the Lord would give you wisdom, too. I heard Jehovah Chereb say:

You are My weapon of war, but it's still My battle. So I am fighting for you and I will fight through you, but you've got to do it My way. You've got to wait for My voice. You've got to seek My wisdom. You've got to heed My counsel. So just stand firm and don't move without My Spirit. Don't move ahead of Me. Don't move beyond the bounds of My grace. Don't move beyond the bounds of faith. Don't move beyond the bounds of My love, but continue to do what is right in the eyes of My Spirit.

CHAPTER 9

THE MYSTERY

OF YOUR WAR ASSIGNMENT

Understand and know this: You are a soldier in the army of God. You have a war assignment. You can't do what angels do, but angels can't do what you do. We all have a part to play. Throughout the pages of Scripture, we see God giving war assignments to His people—either directly or through leaders. God spoke to Moses, for example, then Moses spoke to the people in Numbers 31:3-7:

> *So Moses spoke to the people, saying, "Arm some of yourselves for war, and let them go against the Midianites to take vengeance for the Lord on Midian. A thousand from each tribe of all the tribes of Israel you shall send to the war."*
>
> *So there were recruited from the divisions of Israel one thousand from each tribe, twelve thousand armed for war. Then Moses sent them to the war, one thousand from each tribe; he sent them to the war with Phinehas the son of Eleazar the priest, with the holy articles and the signal trumpets in his*

hand. And they warred against the Midianites, just as the Lord commanded Moses, and they killed all the males.

God directly assigned Joshua to lead the children of Israel into the Promised Land. Joshua 8:1-3 reads:

Now the Lord said to Joshua: "Do not be afraid, nor be dismayed; take all the people of war with you, and arise, go up to Ai. See, I have given into your hand the king of Ai, his people, his city, and his land. And you shall do to Ai and its king as you did to Jericho and its king. Only its spoil and its cattle you shall take as booty for yourselves. Lay an ambush for the city behind it." So Joshua arose, and all the people of war, to go up against Ai; and Joshua chose thirty thousand mighty men of valor and sent them away by night.

God assigned Gideon to wage war against the Midianites. In Judges 6:11-14, we read:

Now the Angel of the Lord came and sat under the terebinth tree which was in Ophrah, which belonged to Joash the Abiezrite, while his son Gideon threshed wheat in the winepress, in order to hide it from the Midianites. And the Angel of the Lord appeared to him, and said to him, "The Lord is with you, you mighty man of valor!"

Gideon said to Him, "O my lord, if the Lord is with us, why then has all this happened to us? And where are all His miracles which our fathers told us about, saying, 'Did not the Lord bring us up from Egypt?' But now the Lord has forsaken us and delivered us into the hands of the Midianites."

Then the Lord turned to him and said, "Go in this might of yours, and you shall save Israel from the hand of the Midianites. Have I not sent you?"

Ecclesiastes 3:8 tells us there is a time of war and a time of peace. There is a season when kings go to war (see 2 Sam. 11:1). You have to discern the season. For many, the season is now. I heard the Lord reciting Joel 3:9: "Proclaim this among the nations: 'Prepare for war! Wake up the mighty men, let all the men of war draw near, let them come up.'"

DISCERNING YOUR WAR ASSIGNMENT

Could God be giving you a war assignment in this season? God doesn't call you to go to war unless you are able to go to war (see Num. 1). Some are young in Christ and not yet trained for battle, but ultimately God wants to use us as a war club in the earth. So how do you discern your war assignment? Keep in mind this is not about the personal spiritual warfare that comes against your mind or your family. This is a broader, strategic level assignment to execute His Kingdom plans in the earth.

There are many different types of war assignments. Some are prophets proclaiming the will of God in the nations. Some are watchmen stationed on the wall and sounding the alarm. Some are intercessors standing in the gap and making up the hedge. Some are evangelists invading new territories with the gospel. Some are teachers making disciples and raising up new spiritual warriors. Some are apostles building and planting. Some are in the marketplace, being salt and light and transferring wealth out of the world and into the Kingdom of God. All of this relates, ultimately, to war.

How do you unravel the mystery of your war assignment? Many times, God will just tell you. Part of my war assignment, for example, is to equip a vast army of warriors for the Kingdom. When the enemy attacks me, I seek wisdom and Jehovah Gibbor's battle plan to overcome for myself—then I share the revelation with the masses so they can overcome. The word of my testimony, then, doesn't just help me overcome but helps you overcome.

Consider this. The U.S. Army hands out war assignments based on talents—skill sets. The Army is not going to send a surgeon to the front lines of battle. The surgeon, instead, will help save the lives of the wounded. The Army is not going to send a journalist to operate in the infirmary. The journalist is assigned to chronicle the war. Likewise, Jehovah Gibbor will assign your place in the war based on how He has gifted you.

First Peter 4:10 tells us, "As each one has received a gift, minister it to one another, as good stewards of the manifold grace of God." And Romans 12:6 says, "Having then gifts differing according to the grace that is given to us, let us use them." Ask Jehovah Gibbor to make this mystery plain to you so that you can be an effective soldier in the army of the Lord. Don't presume to know where to wield your weapons; follow the leading of Jehovah Gibbor. When you do, you will find triumph.

SHALL YOU GO UP?

David understood the battle is the Lord's. That's why he never presumed to take on a battle that wasn't his—and neither should we.

God assigned David to lead the Israelites against the Philistines and other armies, but he waited on the Lord with a question in his heart and a listening ear. That question was: "Shall I go up?"

If God gives us unique battle assignments and offers unique battle plans—and He does—then it only makes sense that not every battle is ours to fight. In our zeal we can feel as if we are unconquerable on the battlefield, but without the grace to fight we will fall. The battle is the Lord's, and He chooses who to send to each skirmish.

God always leads us into triumph (see 2 Cor. 2:14). But if God is not leading us into battle, the triumph is not guaranteed. Ultimately, we win the war but we may get beat down by the enemy's battering ram if we are not graced for the fight. David never lost a battle, and I believe one of the reasons why is because he was careful to ask, "Shall I go up?"

Remember, David was trained for battle in the wilderness. He took out the lion and the bear before he ever went toe to toe with Goliath. His official military career didn't start with a sword and a shield but a sling and a stone. After this great victory, he could have become presumptuous, but he always paused in the face of danger to ask, "Shall I go up?"

I heard Jehovah Gibbor say:

> *Prepare yourself for war. Get ready for the next battle before it rises against you. Press into My strength so you can be strong in Me and the power of My might. Set your forehead like flint and determine to reach your destiny despite the spiritual opposition that will come along your*

path. *My Word is true. Submit yourself to Me. Resist the devil that's resisting you. He will flee. You will accomplish your assignment.*

For I have called you to rise up and push back, to raid the raiders, to go into the enemy's camp and demand justice—to demand repayment. I've called you to rise up and go forward with a confidence that I am with you—that I have sent angel armies before you. I will never let you fight a battle alone. Did I not say I'm always with you? Did I not say I will never forsake you? Did I not say that I would lead you into triumph?

CHAPTER 10

THE MYSTERY
OF ANGEL ARMIES

I saw the Lord sitting on His throne, and all the whole heavenly army was standing by Him at His right hand and His left. God was talking to the angel armies, looking for someone to go down and entice Ahab to march to his death at Ramoth Gilead. The discussion went on for a few minutes before a spirit spoke up and volunteered to become a lying spirit in the mouths of Ahab's prophets.

That wasn't my experience, but Micaiah did see this exact vision of the angel armies in heaven (see 1 Kings 22:19-22). It's been said God works in mysterious ways. If that's true, it's perhaps even more true of His angels. These curious spirit creatures are unseen, yet they are all around us. These invisible warriors are wonderous in their ways as they fly through the heavens and earth faster than the speed of thought executing their Christ-driven mission.

The Bible leaves a shroud of mystery around the angel armies. Angel armies were created before Elohim formed the foundations of the earth—and before He created man in His own image. These angel armies are unseen spirits that appear only when God sends them on assignment or opens our eyes to the seer dimensions. We know they serve at the pleasure of the Captain of the Hosts. Jesus said the angel armies are at His disposal (see Matt. 26:53).

In my epic vision, I, too, saw Jehovah Gibbor handing out battle assignments to the angels present in the war room. These mighty warrior angels were standing at attention with their chests out and their heads up waiting for the word from the Captain of the Hosts. One by one, Jehovah Gibbor dispatched the ministering spirits with unique assignments. One by one, they descended from heaven's war room to the second heaven battleground.

All angels are not created equal—and they don't all have the same assignment. Warring angels are angels with a heaven-charged duty to war with and for you against dark forces that stand against Jehovah Gibbor's will. These warring angels have supernatural strength beyond human capabilities and have sworn allegiance to the Creator God.

Beyond the archangel Michael, we also see warring angels at work in Second Kings 19:35: "And it came to pass on a certain night that the angel of the Lord went out, and killed in the camp of the Assyrians one hundred and eighty-five thousand; and when people arose early in the morning, there were the corpses—all dead." Did you catch that? One angel took out one hundred and eighty-five thousand men! This is a mystery.

In the epic war room vision, Jehovah Gibbor sent one warring angel to fight death, one to fight disease, and one to fight Jezebel. I believe these were the chief angels of a company that would follow them into battle. It seems Jehovah Gibbor was dispatching angels before believers as forerunners to war in the second heaven in response to the declarations of the believers on earth.

ANGELS ASSIGNED TO NATIONS

Again, I did not see all the angels present or hear all of what the heavenly host was assigned to do. Some of these realities were sealed from my view of things to come. However, I had a knowing in my spirit that some of the many angels gathered for marching orders were assigned to nations—some to war against principalities and others to bring judgment.

We know angels can be assigned to nations. Daniel 12:1 tells us, "And at that time Michael shall stand up, the great prince who stands guard over the sons of your people" (MEV). Michael was assigned to Israel. Angels can be assigned to guard nations. At the same time, fallen angels—or principalities—can be assigned over nations as well. These are also called territorial spirits.

In the Book of Daniel, a battle between Michael and an evil angel working to thwart the delivery of his prayer answer is revealed. Daniel 10:12-13 reads:

> *Then he said to me, "Do not be afraid, Daniel. For from the first day that you set your heart to understand this and to humble yourself before your God, your words were heard, and I have come because of your words. But the prince of the kingdom of Persia withstood me for twenty-one days. So*

> *Michael, one of the chief princes, came to help me, for I had been left there with the kings of Persia"* (MEV).

Beyond this dramatic account from the prophet's pen, Scripture also reveals angels are involved in the affairs of Greece. In Daniel 10:20, the prophet's encounter with an angel continues: "Then he said, 'Do you know why I have come to you? And now I must return to fight with the prince of Persia; and when I have gone forth, indeed the prince of Greece will come.'"

Tim Sheets, author of *Angel Armies*, says angelic activity will now increase dramatically. He has seen an increase of angelic activity in his own life and has completed a comprehensive study of angels over the past decade. Indeed, angel armies are responding to the Word of God declared in the earth.

> Also, the Word of God is now being released in faith decrees as never before. Millions of them. This is activating angels to assist Holy Spirit to bring them to pass. In 2007 as Holy Spirit began to download a revelation concerning angel armies. He spoke this to me, "The greatest days in church history are not in your past, they are in your present and your future." To see those days increased angel activity is a must.

Angelic activity—including the angel armies—is a sign of the end times. I write extensively about this in my book *Angels on Assignment Again*.

We must remember this truth as we work with ministry spirits: God commands angels. Humans do not command angels. Psalm

103:20 tells us, "Bless the Lord, you His angels, who are mighty, and do His commands, and obey the voice of His word" (MEV). The New Living Translation of that verse reads: "Praise the Lord, you angels, you mighty ones who carry out his plans, listening for each of his commands." And *The Message* reads, "Bless God, all you armies of angels, alert to respond to whatever he wills. Bless God, all creatures, wherever you are—everything and everyone made by God."

Jesus is the head of the angels now. Second Thessalonians 1:7 speaks of Jesus and His powerful angels. Matthew 24:31 tells us Jesus will send out his angels with the mighty blast of a trumpet. If Jesus is the head of all principalities and powers—and He is—then He is also in charge of the angels (see Col. 2:10). That said, when we decree His Word out of our mouth, it releases angelic activity as they respond the earthly voice-activation of His will in heaven.

ANGEL ARMIES IN ACTION

Angel armies never sleep. Angel armies are intelligent troops dispatched with a word and have wisdom in battle. Second Samuel 14:20 speaks of the wisdom of angels. Angel armies don't lose their breath in the midst of a spiritual wrestling match. Angel armies have supernatural strength. Second Thessalonians 1:7 says they are mighty, and Revelation 18:1 tells us they have great power. Psalm 103:20 says they excel in strength. Consider the account in Second Kings 19:30-35, in which God sends angel armies to fight for the remnant.

"And the remnant who have escaped of the house of Judah shall again take root downward, And bear fruit upward. For

out of Jerusalem shall go a remnant, and those who escape from Mount Zion. The zeal of the Lord of hosts will do this."

Therefore thus says the Lord concerning the king of Assyria: "He shall not come into this city, nor shoot an arrow there, nor come before it with shield, nor build a siege mound against it. By the way that he came, by the same shall he return; and he shall not come into this city," says the Lord. "For I will defend this city, to save it for My own sake and for My servant David's sake."

And it came to pass on a certain night that the angel of the Lord went out, and killed in the camp of the Assyrians one hundred and eighty-five thousand; and when people arose early in the morning, there were the corpses—all dead.

In Elisha's day, the king of Syria was warring against Israel. The prophet Elisha gave the Israelites a marked advantage—he was able to hear the words Syria's king spoke in his bedroom and relayed them to the king of Israel (see 2 Kings 6:12). The Syrian king wanted Elisha stopped and sent out horses and chariots and a great army to fetch him. When Elisha's servant saw the Syrian army surrounding the city, he got scared.

And his servant said to him, "Alas, my master! What shall we do?" So he answered, "Do not fear, for those who are with us are more than those who are with them." And Elisha prayed, and said, "Lord, I pray, open his eyes that he may see." Then the Lord opened the eyes of the young man, and he saw. And behold, the mountain was full of horses and chariots of fire all around Elisha (2 Kings 6:15-17).

SEEING THE ANGEL ARMY

In his book *Angel Armies: Releasing the Warriors of Heaven*, Sheets tells the story of ministering at a church in Jacksonville. He arrived late, but when he walked in he sensed God's supernatural activity was stirring in the worship service.

> As I walked from the back to the front of the auditorium, I began to see flashes of light going back and forth across the congregation. I stopped in my tracks because, as I have taught, that refers to angelic activity. Angels were moving all around the auditorium, ministering to God's people...
>
> The next morning began as the worship leader opened with a song to gather everyone together and prepare their minds for receiving mode. My brother, Dutch Sheets, opened the service in prayer. I stood there on the front row, getting ready to minister, when I saw, off to the right, a group of angels. To the left there was a group of angels stationed as well. They were angel warriors. I looked up and saw angel warriors stationed everywhere![1]

This, of course, was enough to capture his attention but even more so because something similar had happened a few months before in New York. Sheets reports seeing two bands of angels on each side of those who had been called to the altar after Cindy Jacobs called teenagers and adults up to the age of 30 up for prayer.

MAHANAIM MARCHING

> While we were praying, I heard, called out from behind me, "Mahanaim." I know exactly what Mahanaim is because I teach about it. Of course, God knew that that word would grab my attention and I would recognize it meant the Angel of the Lord who accompanies the apostolic assignment on my life. Finally I looked to see who was yelling, "Mahanaim." To my surprise, there was nobody behind me. I began to shake internally.[2]

Mahanaim is a Hebrew word found in Genesis 32. Jacob left Laban to return home and was going to meet his brother Esau, whose birthright he stole. Scripture records Jacob witnessing two groups of angels protecting his family. Jacob called that place Mahanaim, which means "the place of two camps," according to Strong's Concordance.

> Back to the meeting in Jacksonville: I remembered what I had seen in New York and what I had read in Genesis 28. I saw the same thing and I knew the Holy Spirit was using the angels to protect what He is doing with the coming generation—particularly that night, what He was doing with the youth in that church.... I have now had two encounters with *Mahanaim*, seeing them surround, as guards, the next generation.[3]

ANGELS TO COMBAT DEATH AND DISEASE

In my epic vision of the war room in heaven, you'll recall I saw assignments handed out to angels. One was sent to fight death and the other was sent to fight disease. We see an angel operating to stop death and disease in Second Samuel 24. David took a census and grieved the Lord. Jehovah sent Gad to correct David and give the king an opportunity to choose his own punishment. David chose a plague over fleeing from his enemies for three months or seven years of famine. Second Samuel 24:15-17 tells the story:

> *So the Lord sent a plague upon Israel from the morning till the appointed time. From Dan to Beersheba seventy thousand men of the people died. And when the angel stretched out His hand over Jerusalem to destroy it, the Lord relented from the destruction, and said to the angel who was destroying the people, "It is enough; now restrain your hand." And the angel of the Lord was by the threshing floor of Araunah the Jebusite.*
>
> *Then David spoke to the Lord when he saw the angel who was striking the people, and said, "Surely I have sinned, and I have done wickedly; but these sheep, what have they done? Let Your hand, I pray, be against me and against my father's house."*

God is not sending plagues on His people, but He can send angels to combat natural and man-made plagues in the earth to protect His people. I believe He is already doing just that. Notice, too, something remarkable about the mystery of prayer. God had already sent the angel to stop the plague and resulting death before David ever prayed. This is biblical. God said, "Before they call, I will answer; and while they are still speaking, I will hear" (Isa. 65:24).

Beyond disease that brings death, there's the spirit of death itself that is raging in the nations. Macrotrends data shows the death rate is increasing in the world. The spirit of death hearkens to the power of death we release through our mouths (see Prov. 18:21). The wages of sin is death (see Rom. 6:23). And Hebrews 2:14-15 tells us the devil holds the power of death:

> So then, as the children share in flesh and blood, He likewise took part in these, so that through death He might destroy him who has the power of death, that is, the devil, and deliver those who through fear of death were throughout their lives subject to bondage (MEV).

Jesus is the resurrection and the life. His Spirit dwells within you. One of our safeguards against the spirit of death that is rising is to speak words of life. Angels hearken to the voice of God's Word in your mouth (see Ps. 103:4). When you prophesy life over yourself, angels will combat the spirit of death and crush its diabolical assignment to take you out before your time by the words of your mouth.

THE MYSTERY OF ANGELIC RANKS

One hundred eighty-five thousand dead at the hand of a single angel. This is part of the mystery of the angel armies, which leads us to the mystery of angelic ranks. If there is a hierarchy of demons—and there is—there is also a hierarchy of angels. Satan's highly organized kingdom merely mimics the glorious Kingdom of heaven.

Although different commenters throughout church history have offered different takes on the ranks of angels, we know ranks exist. We can see this reality in Daniel 10. Daniel saw a vision and ended up in a deep sleep, with his face to the ground, when suddenly he felt a hand touch him. At that, he climbed to his knees with his palms to the ground and trembled. It was a warrior angel—a member of the angel armies—with a message. Read Daniel 10:11-14:

> *And he said to me, "O Daniel, man greatly beloved, understand the words that I speak to you, and stand upright, for I have now been sent to you." While he was speaking this word to me, I stood trembling. Then he said to me, "Do not fear, Daniel, for from the first day that you set your heart to understand, and to humble yourself before your God, your words were heard; and I have come because of your words. But the prince of the kingdom of Persia withstood me twenty-one days; and behold, Michael, one of the chief princes, came to help me, for I had been left alone there with the kings of Persia. Now I have come to make you understand what will happen to your people in the latter days, for the vision refers to many days yet to come."*

If some angels weren't more powerful than others—if some angels didn't rank higher—the angel who spoke to Daniel would not have needed help from Michael, the archangel. The angel who spoke to Daniel was of a lower rank than the principality he was fighting. When Michael came on the scene, the battle no doubt ended quickly.

DOES DIONYSIUS INTERPRET MYSTERY?

Pseudo-Dionysius, a Christian philosopher of the late 5th century, offers prophetic insight into the mystery of angelic ranks. His philosophy, which draws on Bible passages, is offered in the book *De Coelesti Hierarchia*. In it, he describes angels ranked into three hierarchies and nine orders. As he explains it, the first hierarchy contains seraphim, cherubim, and thrones. The second hierarchy contains dominions, virtues, and powers. And the third hierarchy contains principalities, archangels, and angels.

Seeing the Seraphim

Pseudo-Dionysius ranked seraphim as the highest order of angels. Isaiah saw the seraphim during his commissioning:

> *In the year that King Uzziah died, I saw the Lord sitting on a throne, high and lifted up, and the train of His robe filled the temple. Above it stood seraphim; each one had six wings: with two he covered his face, with two he covered his feet, and with two he flew. And one cried to another and said: "Holy, holy, holy is the Lord of hosts; the whole earth is full of His glory!"* (Isaiah 6:1-3)

Strong's Concordance defines seraphim as majestic beings with six wings and human hands or voices in attendance upon God. You might say these are God's armorbearers who take care of His throne room. It was a seraph God sent with a coal he took from the altar to put to Isaiah's mouth (see Isa. 6:6). But I did not see seraphim at the table in my epic war room vision.

Cherubim Flank God's Throne

Cherubim are second in the first order of angels. Strong's defines cherubim as angelic beings that flank God's throne. Cherubim were imaged hovering over the Ark of the Covenant. God sent the cherubim on an important mission after the fall of man. We see cherubim in the Book of Beginnings. Genesis 3:22-24 reads:

> *Then the Lord God said, "Behold, the man has become like one of Us, to know good and evil. And now, lest he put out his hand and take also of the tree of life, and eat, and live forever"—therefore the Lord God sent him out of the garden of Eden to till the ground from which he was taken. So He drove out the man; and He placed cherubim at the east of the garden of Eden, and a flaming sword which turned every way, to guard the way to the tree of life.*

We see cherubim appear sixty-six times in Scripture, including many instances of this description: "the Lord of Hosts, who dwells between the cherubim" (2 Sam. 6:2). Ezekiel had a dramatic vision of the cherubim as the glory of God departed from the temple in Ezekiel 10. But I did not see seraphim at the table in my epic war room vision.

Thrones, Good, and Evil

Colossians 1:16 reveals, "For by Him all things were created that are in heaven and that are on earth, visible and invisible, whether thrones or dominions or principalities or powers. All things were created through Him and for Him." There are good thrones and evil thrones.

The word *throne* in that verse comes from the Greek word *thronos*, which means "a throne seat, a chair of state having a footstool." But it also refers to a plural of angels in Colossians 1:16, according to *Thayer's Greek Lexicon*. We know that Christ's enemies will one day be made a footstool under His feet (see Heb. 10:13). Right now, some of them are sitting on demonic thrones. But I did not see thrones at the table in my epic war room vision.

Dealing with Dominions

Colossians 1:16 also speaks of dominions. *Strong's* defines *kuriotes*, the Greek word for *dominions*, as "divine or angelic lordship, domination, dignity, usually with reference to a celestial hierarchy." HELPS Word Studies offers a slightly different definition: "a power exerting itself in a particular jurisdiction."[4] Ephesians 1:21 speaks of Christ being far above principality, and power, and might, and dominion. But I did not see dominions at the table in my epic war room vision.

Virtues

In line with Jewish angelic hierarchies, Pseudo-Dionysius and St. Thomas Aquinas in his *Summa Theologica* speak of virtues and point to the relation with the Greek word *dunamis* in Ephesians 1:21. One of Strong's definitions of *dunamis* is "power consisting in or resting upon armies, forces, and hosts." They believed these angels work with God in signs and miracles in the world. But I did not see virtues at the table in my epic war room vision.

Powers

The Greek word for *powers* in this verse is *exousia*, which means "power, authority, weight, especially: moral authority, influence." We see an angel in the Book of Revelation who has the power of fire (see Rev. 14:18). In Revelation 18:1 an angel came down from heaven with great power and lit up the earth with his glory. Revelation 16:5 speaks of the angels of the waters. But I did not see powers at the table in my epic war room vision.

Principalities

According to *The KJV New Testament Greek Lexicon*, the word *principality* comes from the Greek word *arche*. In Ephesians 6:12, the word *principalities* refers to "the first place, principality, rule, magistracy" and speaks of "angels and demons." *Vine's Expository Dictionary* reveals that it is used of "supramundane beings who exercise rule." *Merriam-Webster* defines principality as "the state, office, or authority of a prince" and "the territory or jurisdiction of a prince: the country that gives title to a prince." I saw principalities in the war room.

Archangels

The most famed archangel—and the only one in the Bible—is Michael. Archangels contend with demons (see Jude 9). When Jesus returns, an archangel will shout (see 1 Thess. 4:16). The Greek word for *archangel* is *archaggelos*—it means "chief angels." Pseudo-Dionysius ranks them toward the bottom, but this seems to mean the archangel is the chief of the warring angels. I saw archangels in the war room.

Angels

The Greek word for *angel*—*angelos*—in the New Testament takes on the masculine form and there is no corresponding feminine form of the word. Angels are essentially messengers. I saw warring angels in the war room.

COOPERATING WITH ANGEL ARMIES

As mighty as David was in battle—after all, he defeated Goliath with a sling and a stone when the rest of the children of Israel were shaking in their boots and sang songs about how he slew tens of thousands (see 1 Sam. 18:7)—he still called on angels of war in times of distress. David prayed to the Lord to send angels on assignment to fight for him in war in Psalm 35. You'll notice how David depends on the Lord, but calls for the angels.

> *Plead my cause, O Lord, with my adversaries; fight those who fight me. Take hold of the large shield and small shield, and rise up for my help. Draw the spear and javelin against those who pursue me. Say to my soul, "I am Your salvation." May those who seek my life be ashamed and humiliated; may those who plan my injury be turned back and put to shame. May they be as chaff before the wind, and may the angel of the Lord cast them down. May their way be dark and slippery, and may the angel of the Lord pursue them. For without cause they have hidden their net for me in a pit, which they have dug without cause for my soul* (Psalm 35:1-7 MEV).

Jesus Himself mentioned angels in the context of war on the night of His betrayal in the Garden of Gethsemane. Peter's first response to the soldiers trying to take Jesus into custody was to pull out his sword and fight. But Jesus corrected him in Matthew 26:52-54:

> *Then Jesus said to him, "Put your sword back in its place. For all those who take up the sword will perish by the sword. Do you think that I cannot now pray to My Father, and He will at once give Me more than twelve legions of angels? But how then would the Scriptures be fulfilled, that it must be so?"* (MEV)

The weapons of our warfare are not carnal, but mighty in God for pulling down strongholds (see 2 Cor. 10:4). Angels are not weapons, but they are on God's side and God is for us. If God is for us, who can be against us? God has given us authority to bind and loose in the name of Jesus (see Rom. 8:31; Matt. 16:19), but there are times when He will send angels to help us in battle.

ANGEL ARMY ACTIVITY RISING

Sheets says angelic activity will now increase dramatically. He has seen an increase of angelic activity in his own life, and has completed a comprehensive study of angels over the past decade.

> Angels assist Holy Spirit and the heirs of salvation (Heb. 1:14) to do God's will upon the earth. They work to enforce the decrees of God's Word (Psalm 103:20). We

are living in the season of the greatest move of God in history. Angels are needed to help facilitate that move," Sheets says.

Also, the Word of God is now being released in faith decrees as never before. Millions of them. This is activating angels to assist Holy Spirit to bring them to pass. In 2007 as Holy Spirit began to download a revelation concerning angel armies. He spoke this to me, "The greatest days in church history are not in your past, they are in your present and your future." To see those days increased angel activity is a must.

THE MYSTERY OF A SAINTS-AND-ANGELS ARMY

Throughout the pages of Scripture, we see angel armies in action, though they remain a mystery many heavenly minded believers long to look into. Jesus told us He was coming back with angel armies (see Matt. 25:31). At the Second Coming, some will see the angel armies in action. John had an apocalyptic vision that included the angel armies. Read the dramatic account in Revelation 19:11-16:

> *Now I saw heaven opened, and behold, a white horse. And He who sat on him was called Faithful and True, and in righteousness He judges and makes war. His eyes were like a flame of fire, and on His head were many crowns. He had a name written that no one knew except Himself. He was*

clothed with a robe dipped in blood, and His name is called The Word of God. And the armies in heaven, clothed in fine linen, white and clean, followed Him on white horses. Now out of His mouth goes a sharp sword, that with it He should strike the nations. And He Himself will rule them with a rod of iron. He Himself treads the winepress of the fierceness and wrath of Almighty God. And He has on His robe and on His thigh a name written: KING OF KINGS AND LORD OF LORDS.

These armies in heaven include saints and angels. Could it be possible that some of the angels and saints whom I saw in my epic vision are part of this end-times entourage? Could it be possible David will lead his mighty men? Could Gideon lead his army of 300—or 300,000,000? Will Joshua lead some of the remnant Israelites who went on to glory? Will Abraham lead the 318 servant warriors trained in his own household? I believe that is very possible, which is why I saw many of these figures at the war room conference table with the angels.

THE MYSTERY OF CHRIST'S ANGELIC PARTNERSHIP

Then there's the mystery of why Jesus brings the angel armies. He is Almighty God. Technically, He could snap His fingers and the war would be over. What is the purpose of the angel armies?

Jesus historically received the ministry of angels while He walked the earth. When He was in the wilderness, the angels strengthened

Him. Angels also ministered to Jesus in the Garden of Gethsemane. I believe angels were part and parcel of Christ's ministry when He walked the earth in ways that are not revealed in Scripture. But why does Jesus come back with angel armies? Revelation 19:19-21 tells us more about the end-times war.

> *And I saw the beast, the kings of the earth, and their armies, gathered together to make war against Him who sat on the horse and against His army. Then the beast was captured, and with him the false prophet who worked signs in his presence, by which he deceived those who received the mark of the beast and those who worshiped his image. These two were cast alive into the lake of fire burning with brimstone. And the rest were killed with the sword which proceeded from the mouth of Him who sat on the horse. And all the birds were filled with their flesh.*

Here is the mystery unraveled—the angel armies in the end times become ministers of justice. God doesn't need them to protect Him in the battle. No weapon formed against the risen Christ shall prosper. The angel armies will avenge the saints on the great and terrible day of the Lord. Second Thessalonians 1:6-10 reveals this mystery:

> *And God will provide rest for you who are being persecuted and also for us when the Lord Jesus appears from heaven. He will come with his mighty angels, in flaming fire, bringing judgment on those who don't know God and on those who refuse to obey the Good News of our Lord Jesus. They will be punished with eternal destruction, forever separated from the Lord and from his glorious power. When he comes on*

that day, he will receive glory from his holy people—praise from all who believe. And this includes you, for you believed what we told you about him (NLT).

A WORD FROM THE CAPTAIN OF THE HOSTS

I heard the Captain of the Hosts say:

I'm sending angelic assistance your way. I'm dispatching to you angels on assignment just for you. I'm releasing the angels of breakthrough into your life. Don't stop praying now. The angels are coming on assignment because of your words. Don't shrink back from the battle. Help from the heavenly host is on the way. Don't pull back and don't cease fire. You are on the brink of victory. Don't let your foot off the gas. You are speeding forth into triumph. Keep pressing. Keep praying. Angels are encamped around you even now because you fear Me.

Send the word forth out of your mouth. Send My word out of your mouth and watch the angels come, even the breakthrough angels come to help you, to assist you, to break through the opposition in the spirit that you cannot see. You discern that it's there, but you cannot see it. You understand because you keep bumping into it, but you don't know how to move it. And even though you've tried to cast the opposition into the sea, your faith has faltered, and you've grown weary in well doing. So, just keep speaking the Word only and watch Me move. Watch the angels go. Watch the demons flee.

NOTES

1. Tim Sheets, *Angel Armies* (Shippensburg, PA: Destiny Image Publishers, 2016), 26-27.

2. Ibid., 27.

3. Ibid., 28-29.

4. HELPS Word-studies, "2963 kuriotés," accessed on Biblehub .com, https://biblehub.com/greek/2963.htm.

CHAPTER 11

THE MYSTERY
OF WARRING AGAINST PRINCIPALITIES

In the Book of Revelation, we read about an epic war between good and evil—a battle between the archangel Michael and his angels and a cohort of demons. The dramatic account is recorded in Revelation 12:6-8, demonstrating the warring nature of some angels on assignment.

> *The woman fled into the wilderness where she has a place prepared by God, that they may nourish her there for one thousand two hundred and sixty days. Then war broke out in heaven. Michael and his angels fought against the dragon, and the dragon and his angels fought, but they did not prevail, nor was there a place for them in heaven any longer* (MEV).

Michael warred against principalities—but should we? A common question—or let's call it a debate—among believers and even leaders in the Body of Christ is, "Should we battle principalities?" It's downright controversial and it's a loaded question. John Paul Jackson, a prophetic voice who went home to be with the Lord in 2015, argued strongly against waging war in the second heaven—or battling principalities. Based on revelation from a dream, his book *Needless Casualties of War* continues to make his case after his passing.

Jackson's book asserts presumption led to needless casualties because Christians do not have the authority to battle principalities, also called territorial demons. Christians, he writes, are authorized for ground level warfare. He says he received a revelation from the Lord that Christians are dying, getting sick, and falling because they are going on the offense against principalities. In his view, we battle territorial spirits through repenting of words, thoughts, and deeds that give them a legal right. After repentance, he suggests, we ask God to deal with them.

> I have adopted a more conservative perspective on spiritual warfare—one that allows me to distinguish between warfare in a terrestrial arena from warfare in a second Heaven arena. It is my belief that unless you understand the parameters of our delegated authority and some practical guidelines on how to properly engage in spiritual warfare, there's a strong possibility that you could become an unfortunate victim of war. ... We don't have the anointing or the authority to wage war in the heavenly realms. We've only been commissioned to subdue the Earth.[1]

Jackson offers five reasons why we are not to engage spiritual beings in second heaven warfare. First, he says, Christ never did. When the disciples asked Jesus to teach them how to pray in Matthew 6, Jackson explains, he did not instruct them to come after the dark forces in the territory. Jackson emphasizes Christ's teaching to address God rather than heavenly beings.

Second, Jackson points to Jude 8, in which we are advised not to speak evil of celestial dignitaries. Again, Jackson contends man is given authority on earth, not in the heavens. He then points to Jesus' words in Luke 10:19, "Behold, I give you the authority to trample on serpents and scorpions, and over all the power of the enemy, and nothing shall by any means hurt you." Jackson believes this affirms our authority is in the earth realm and not the second heavens.

Finally, Jackson gives as evidence Psalm 8:5—that man is made a little lower than angels. If we are a little lower than angels, he says, we do not carry the authority to tell spiritual beings what to do. But not everyone agrees with Jackson's revelation. In fact, some strongly disagree and offer a different view in Scripture.

ENGAGING IN STRATEGIC-LEVEL WARFARE

Leaders like the late C. Peter Wagner and John Dawson focus their teaching on territorial demons over nations—called strategic-level spiritual warfare—and pushing them back to see the transformation of cities and regions. Nations like Argentina, Colombia, and Fiji have seen miraculous transformations based on their approach.

Wagner and his contemporaries point to Second Corinthians 2:11 in which Paul tells us not to be ignorant of the devil's devices. They also highlight the words of Jesus, who told us we have to bind the strong man in order to plunder his house (see Mark 3:27). Wagner writes:

> The "house" is the territory controlled by Satan, or his delegated spirits, and that territory cannot be taken unless he is bound. But once the territorial spirits are bound, the kingdom of God can flow into the territory and "plunder the strong man's goods," as it were.[2]

Of course, Wagner is not suggesting that individuals take on principalities toe to toe. He writes:

> Work with the intercessors especially gifted and called to strategic-level spiritual warfare, seeking God's revelation of: (a) the redemptive gift(s) of the city; (b) Satan's strongholds; (c) territorial spirits assigned to the city; (d) corporate sin; (e) God's plan of attack and timing.[3]

In her book *Possessing the Gates of the Enemy*, Cindy Jacobs writes:

> God will quicken these prophetic intercessors to pray for and often go to "hot spots." They tear down spiritual strongholds and fight principalities and powers over nations. They make breaches in the enemy's defenses so that God can move in and bring revival or send in missionaries. Just as in a modern-day military strategy, they go in first to prepare the way for the Lord's purposes in the area.[4]

Mike Bickle, director of the International House of Prayer in Kansas City, offers this insight:

How often have you seen overzealous believers approach spiritual warfare with the idea that they are demon-busters out looking for the next satanic stronghold to bring down? They focus almost entirely on the demonic realm and get excited at the mere mention of binding evil spirits, casting out devils and pulling down strongholds. There's a problem with this, however. In most cases spiritual warfare is not to be carried out by directly confronting the powers and principalities over cities and nations. The New Testament model for spiritual warfare is to direct our prayers to God, proclaim His name and promises, and do His works as the primary way to wrestle with the disembodied evil spirits in the heavenly places. These evil spirits are called principalities, powers, rulers of the darkness of this age and spiritual hosts of wickedness (Eph. 6:12). Of course, there are exceptions to this general rule, in which case we address our proclamations directly to the enemy. On specific occasions the Spirit may lead someone to speak directly in intercession to a demonic principality. But this is not the primary prayer model presented by the New Testament apostles.[5]

FINDING THE BALANCE

I do agree we have different levels of authority in the spirit, based in part on our revelation and experience. My thought is this: Always let the Holy Spirit lead you. I'll keep saying this: God always leads us into triumph in Christ Jesus (see 2 Cor. 2:14). The Holy Spirit could lead you take on principalities in a corporate setting, but it's a relatively rare occurrence. In the decades I've walked with the Lord, I have not been led to individually come against principalities. You better be sure the Lord has called you to do this before you embark on this type of warfare, which should always be corporate.

Consider this. Even Michael, the archangel—the warring prince of the angelic army—did not take satan head-on. Jude 9 reveals:

> *But when [even] the archangel Michael, contending with the devil, judicially argued (disputed) about the body of Moses, he dared not [presume to] bring an abusive condemnation against him, but [simply] said, The Lord rebuke you!* (AMPC)

Michael did battle a demonic principality that a fellow, lower-ranking angel could not defeat on his own. After Daniel released his repentance and prayer during Israel's captivity, there was a war in the second heaven to deliver the answer. We read the account in Daniel 10:12-14:

> *Then he said to me, "Do not fear, Daniel, for from the first day that you set your heart to understand, and to humble yourself before your God, your words were heard; and I have come because of your words. But the prince of the kingdom of Persia withstood me twenty-one days; and behold, Michael, one of the chief princes, came to help me, for I had been left alone there with the kings of Persia. Now I have come to*

make you understand what will happen to your people in the latter days, for the vision refers to many days yet to come."

I've also gone against principalities when I shouldn't have and endured heavy attacks. One instance was during the early days of Awakening House of Prayer, my church and international prayer ministry headquartered in Ft. Lauderdale, Florida.

When we walked into the prayer meeting, I sensed it was going to be an all-out war. Of course, the moment we got saved, we enlisted as soldiers in the army of the Lord. We are, indeed, in a war. The enemy of our souls is lurking and looking for an open door to attack. And sometimes his demons don't wait for an open door. They just attack.

The enemy is already a defeated foe. Jesus disarmed principalities and powers, making a public spectacle of them, triumphing over them by His work on the cross (see Col. 2:15). As born-again citizens of heaven, we remain here to enforce Christ's rule in a foreign land. So we effectively live in a war zone.

Jesus gave us authority to trample on serpents and scorpions, and over all the power of the enemy, and nothing shall by any means harm us (see Luke 10:19). But that doesn't mean we don't have to wage spiritual warfare. It just means when we wrestle against principalities, against powers, against the rulers of the darkness of this age, against spiritual hosts of wickedness in the heavenly places (see Eph. 6:12)—when we seek to enforce Christ's rule on this earth, He always leads us into triumph (see 2 Cor. 2:14).

The key word is "leads." I don't believe Jesus leads us to battle principalities alone. I don't believe we are going to pull Jezebel down over a city in a single day. I don't believe principalities can be completely torn down from the second heaven worldwide until Jesus comes back.

All that said, I am not afraid of principalities. I have endured attacks from principalities that were brutal, but I survived. One caution I will give concerns Leviathan. This is a principality Scripture specifically warns us not to tackle. I write more about this in my book *The Spiritual Warrior's Guide to Defeating Water Spirits*:

> Leviathan is not a spirit to stir up. In other words, some weekend warriors tend to start calling out spirits and binding them with bravado. As a principality, Leviathan cannot be bound in the same way you would bind a spirit of fear. It's entrenched in regions and works on the minds of people rather than occupying a place in their souls as rejection or lust might.[6]

I heard the Lord say:

> *Ancient spirits may attack you, but I am the Ancient of Days. I am the Creator of the Universe. I created thrones and principalities and dominions and principalities and powers. I created everything that exists. Ancient spirits have no more authority over you because you are in Me and I am in you. So know that ancestral spirits and ancient spirits must bow to the Ancient of Days on the inside of you. I have prepared you for victory eternal. Eternity past and the spirits that dwelled there have no power over you.*

NOTES

1. John Paul Jackson *Needless Casualties of War* (Streams Publishing House, 2016), 8, 80.

2. C. Peter Wagner, *Engaging the Enemy: How to Fight and Defeat Territorial Spirits* (Ventura, CA: Regal Books, 1991), 280.

3. C. Peter Wagner, *Breaking Strongholds in Your City* (Ventura, CA: Regal Books, 1993), 223-232.

4. Cindy Jacobs, *Possessing the Gates of the Enemy* (Bloomington, MN: Chosen Books, 2018), 85.

5. Mike Bickle, "Praying Down Powers and Principalities," The Vineyard Church, November 28, 2014, http://www .thevineyardfw.org/wordpress/praying-down-powers-and -principalities.

6. Jennifer LeClaire, *The Spiritual Warrior's Guide to Defeating Water Spirits* (Shippensburg, PA: Destiny Image Publishers, 2018), 78.

CHAPTER 12

THE MYSTERY

OF JEZEBEL'S DAUGHTER

I was in a house that was unfamiliar to me. It wasn't a large house, but it was crowded with people—overcrowded. It was almost like a college party house where the living room was over capacity but nobody seemed to mind. Everyone was enjoying themselves, but I could not discern the occasion. I wasn't sure what they were celebrating. It was as if the Holy Spirit picked me up and transported me in the spirit to a faraway place into an event already in progress.

I kept on watching. In this congested home full of Christians, people were running to and fro doing I do not know what. The entire house was buzzing with activity, almost as if they were preparing for something. I could not see the faces of these hectic herds. It was if the Lord was purposely hiding the faces of the people, which I am sure represent a great number of others.

I kept on watching. I did not speak with anyone. I just kept observing and discerning. I was in the room, but it was as if no one could see me. I wasn't sure if I was invisible or if they just didn't notice me. Either way, I was glad I was seemingly invisible. I was grieved, though I did not yet know why. After some time, I was aware people noticed my presence but carried on anyhow.

I kept on watching. No one really spoke to me except one man. I could not see his face either. Because the man engaged in conversation, my journalism instincts took over and I started asking him questions about what was going on. My soul was investigating my spiritual agitation. I was not sure if it was an angel or the Lord. I did not get an immediate answer.

I kept on watching. It was so surreal yet altogether real. After some time, I discerned the people were confined in this house, though they were seemingly unaware of their imprisonment. They went in willingly and had not yet figured out how difficult it would be to escape. The people remained busy doing many things, but not one of them ever went out. Their movement was limited to inside this house. They had no idea that they were trapped. They could not leave.

A CULT COMPOUND

I kept on watching. As I observed, this house reminded me of a cult compound. The people inside were there of their own free will and actually did not want to leave. Their needs were met. They had fellowship. As I said earlier, it seemed like they were enjoying themselves. They were deceived. Fully deceived. But what had deceived them? What happened? What pathway led them into this house?

I kept on watching. After a while, it was mealtime. Food was being distributed on a platter, just like at a party. It wasn't any kind of food I readily recognized. It was strange. After having blended into the background for some time, I was recognized again. I was offered something to eat from this platter.

I kept on watching. With a better view, I saw it was a strange looking piece of meat on the platter. It was oversized on a large bone—and it was one just a single serving. I thought, "No one could eat all this at one time." Some offered me the meat. I politely declined because it was strange. I instinctively felt that if I ate the meat I would be coming into agreement with whatever was going on there.

I kept on watching. As I looked on, I was disturbed in my spirit as other people accepted this strange food. It was almost like it was a matter of survival, because the food that was being offered was the only food available. Yet no one thought it strange. They welcomed it. They devoured it as if it were a filet mignon. Yet I would not eat it. I could not eat it.

RED ALERT

I kept on watching. Suddenly, the party seemed to end. Everyone in the house was on high alert. I could not perceive any immediate danger, but people were scrambling around as if something bad were about to happen. I separated myself. I walked down a hall and went into a bedroom. There was an oversized window in the bedroom.

I kept on watching. As I looked outside the window, I saw two women in a car pulling into the driveway. I suddenly knew this was what was causing the alarm in the house. I bent down to stay out of view and kept peeking through the window.

I kept on watching. The two women were carrying something into the house. I could not see them and did not want them to see me. I was trying to discern what was happening. I felt alarmed in my spirit and my adrenaline was flowing. Finally, they saw me. They wanted me to open the door to the house and let them in. Everyone else was hiding. I was the only one who seemed positioned or even willing to let them in. I decided it was safe, that they presented no danger to me, and set out to let them in. Then I woke up.

JEZEBEL UNLEASHED

When I woke up, I realized this dream was not about me, but the Lord was showing me something about the Body of Christ and my role in the situation. After years of praying into this, I have resolved at least part of the interpretation.

I was an observer in the dream, which means I was standing as an intercessor. Houses in dreams often represent ministry. This was a communal house rather than an individual's home. This was a false camp within the prophetic movement that had been deceived by Jezebel. In other words, these were Jezebel's prophets. I did not recognize the house in the dream because I had never been in it.

The Bible speaks of the prophets of Jezebel. As I wrote in my book *Discerning Prophetic Witchcraft*, prophets of Jezebel are influenced by the spirit of Ashtoreth. Ashtoreth was the pagan god Queen Jezebel served. Ashtoreth was known as a seducing goddess of war. The prophets of Jezebel prophesy smooth, flattering words to try to manipulate and control you. If that doesn't work, they transition into warfare mode and prophesy fearful sayings to try to intimidate and control you. Ashtoreth and Baal were married. So these spirits often share one another's characteristics. We must discern what we are dealing with.

Lester Sumrall once said Jezebel was one of the main spirits the end-times church would have to contend with. It's no coincidence that Jezebel shows up in the Book of Revelation. And it's no accident that the epic war room vision I saw revealed that God was going to dispatch angels to fight death, disease, and Jezebel. Prophetically speaking, I believe the angels fighting death and disease are doing so on behalf of believers in the face of coming plagues. I believe the angels battling Jezebel are coming near the end.

THAT WOMAN JEZEBEL

Jesus left a letter for the church at Thyatira. He wrote these words that we must understand if we want to resist the influence of Jezebel. We read this important, relevant letter in Revelation 2:18-29:

> *These things says the Son of God, who has eyes like a flame of fire, and His feet like fine brass: "I know your works, love, service, faith, and your patience; and as for your works, the last are more than the first. Nevertheless*

I have a few things against you, because you allow that woman Jezebel, who calls herself a prophetess, to teach and seduce My servants to commit sexual immorality and eat things sacrificed to idols. And I gave her time to repent of her sexual immorality, and she did not repent. Indeed I will cast her into a sickbed, and those who commit adultery with her into great tribulation, unless they repent of their deeds. I will kill her children with death, and all the churches shall know that I am He who searches the minds and hearts. And I will give to each one of you according to your works.

"Now to you I say, and to the rest in Thyatira, as many as do not have this doctrine, who have not known the depths of Satan, as they say, I will put on you no other burden. But hold fast what you have till I come. And he who overcomes, and keeps My works until the end, to him I will give power over the nations—'He shall rule them with a rod of iron; they shall be dashed to pieces like the potter's vessels'—as I also have received from My Father; and I will give him the morning star. He who has an ear, let him hear what the Spirit says to the churches."

The spirit of Jezebel is real and raging. It has infiltrated some camps of the prophetic movement. We must stay pure. Purity is one of the key defenses against the Jezebel spirit. Where there are unhealed hurts and wounds, they can fester and bring bitterness that attracts Jezebel to be your protector. Prophetically speaking, now is the time to get free from every tie that binds because the warfare is only going to increase in the days ahead.

EATING AT JEZEBEL'S TABLE

After much prayer, I believe the man who spoke to me was an angel. He seemed to be an ally in the house. I inquired of the angel in the dream for explanations, just like prophets in the Bible inquired of angels in their epic visions. I cannot remember what he said. I believe part of that revelation was withheld for another time.

I understand the strange food is food that was coming from Jezebel's table. When Elijah called for the showdown at Mount Carmel, he instructed Ahab, "Now therefore, send and gather all Israel to me on Mount Carmel, the four hundred and fifty prophets of Baal, and the four hundred prophets of Asherah, who eat at Jezebel's table" (1 Kings 18:19).

Just as there were prophets who ate at Jezebel's table in the original false prophetic movement, there are prophets who eat at Jezebel's table in today's false prophetic movement. Thank God there is a remnant, but the false prophetic camp is feeding right on the doctrines of satan Jesus mentioned in the Book of Revelation.

The house in the dream was unfamiliar to me because whatever this prophetic camp is, I have not been up close to it. I have seen a lot of false prophetic functions over the last decades, but whatever this is I have yet to see it closely enough to describe it. Then again, I could not see the people's faces. They could be people we all recognize or people who have not yet made it onto the scene. I hope I never do see the fullness of this dream manifest, but we know Jesus prophesied false prophets would rise in the last days and deceive many. There is no praying away this reality.

STRANGE FOOD, STRANGE FIRE

Any time I am offered food in a dream I won't eat it. In this particular dream, the meat represented revelation as a reward for compromising with Jezebel. Remember, the false prophets who ate at her table were living it up in a time of famine. They were on Jezebel's payroll. They were Jezebel's yes-men. The true prophets were either dead at Jezebel's hands, escaped to other countries, hiding in a cave eating bread, or roaming about like Elijah.

Keep in mind, meals in the Bible often represent provision, covenant, and even an intimacy in sharing. The people in this home had made a covenant with Jezebel and she was providing for them—a house and food. They had established a level of intimacy with Jezebel. The meat, again, is revelation, but what about the bone? A bone in a dream can often represent something that has no spiritual life.

This strange food also represented strange fire. We see the concept of strange fire in Leviticus 10:1-2: "And Nadab and Abihu, the sons of Aaron, took either of them his censer, and put fire therein, and put incense thereon, and offered strange fire before the Lord, which he commanded them not. And there went out fire from the Lord, and devoured them, and they died before the Lord" (KJV). This was a fatal sin.

What is this strange fire? Strange fire is unauthorized fire. Other translations call it the wrong kind of fire, profane fire, and unholy fire. Aaron's sons did not get their fire from the holy altar of God. Strange fire is more than prophesying out of the soul and innocently thinking it's God. Strange fire "implies not only that they did it of their own proper motion, without any command or authority from God, but that they did it against his command," according to *Benson's Commentary*.

A WARNING OF JUDGMENT

In my dream, there was some sort of alarm in the house. The people started to scatter. I believe it was a warning of coming judgment. God judged the strange fire and He will judge Jezebel. Jesus said He will throw her on a sick bed, along with those who commit adultery with her (see Rev. 2:22). These prophets were eating from Jezebel's table and operating in strange fire. Judgment must come, but the time is not yet.

I went into the bedroom, a place of intimacy in a house full of chaos. No one else was there. Intimacy with Jesus will help us avoid the snares of Jezebel. In the dream, I looked through a window, which in dream language often speaks of prophetic perspective. I had seen what is in the living room of the house. From my secret place, looking through a window, I was seeing what is to come.

What puzzled me was the two women pulling into the driveway. I prayed and pondered this and suddenly the Lord took me to Zechariah 5. What unfolded next took my breath away. I believe the two women represented spirit beings like in Zechariah 5. They were intent on getting in the house and they carried something.

ZECHARIAH'S STARTLING VISION

The following is the account from Zechariah 5:5-11:

> *Then the angel who was talking with me came forward and said, "Look up and see what's coming." "What is it?" I*

asked. He replied, "It is a basket for measuring grain, and it's filled with the sins of everyone throughout the land." Then the heavy lead cover was lifted off the basket, and there was a woman sitting inside it. The angel said, "The woman's name is Wickedness," and he pushed her back into the basket and closed the heavy lid again. Then I looked up and saw two women flying toward us, gliding on the wind. They had wings like a stork, and they picked up the basket and flew into the sky. "Where are they taking the basket?" I asked the angel. He replied, "To the land of Babylonia, where they will build a temple for the basket. And when the temple is ready, they will set the basket there on its pedestal" (NLT).

As Zechariah meditated on what he saw, an angel of interpretation came forth to help him understand the meaning. Essentially, the angel helped the prophet see how iniquity must be removed from the Holy Land. Consider part of the prophet's ministry is to teach people to separate the profane from the holy (see Ezek. 44:23).

WHO IS THE WOMAN IN THE BASKET?

Who is this woman in the basket? The angel said her name is Wickedness. When I first had the dream, I thought it was Jezebel. I pondered on this dream for the better part of two years because I did not have enough interpretation to release it to the Body of Christ. This is the first time I have spoken or shared it publicly, because I only now see the bigger picture.

Up until now, we've been seeing the prophets of Baal and the prophets of Jezebel. But what is coming as we edge toward the end is even more sinister. In 2018, I underwent one of the most severe, longest-lasting attacks I have ever endured. It was one of the most physically excruciating and the most mentally draining. It was my first major battle with the spirit of Athaliah, Jezebel's daughter. I share more about this in my book *Jezebel's Revenge: Annihilating the Spirit of Athaliah*.

When I first had this dream, I thought perhaps it was Jezebel in the basket. But no, it's a spirit more wicked than even the notorious Jezebel. It's the spirit of Athaliah in the basket. Meredith G. Kline confirms this in Kerux, a publication devoted to biblical theology. She also shares this confirmation in her book *Glory in Our Midst*. "Surely this embodiment of wickedness in the apostate Athaliah is the historical model behind Zechariah's image of wickedness personified as the woman in the ephah," she writes.[1]

Jezebel is quite literally the mother of harlots John writes about in Revelation 17:1-6. Athaliah is one of the most wicked harlots in the Bible. Indeed, Athaliah is more wicked than Jezebel, carrying the traits of her father Ahab—who did more to provoke the Lord to anger than any king before him (see 1 Kings 16:33)—and Jezebel.

JEZEBEL'S REVENGE

The wicked Queen Jezebel died at the hand of her eunuchs after Jehu rode furiously toward her dwelling and commanded them to "throw her down" (2 Kings 9:33). But the spirit that was influencing

Jezebel sought revenge. That spirit found revenge through Jezebel and Ahab's daughter, Athaliah. She became the first-ever queen of Israel by murdering all other royal heirs to the throne. Only one, Jehoash, escaped.

According to *Smith's Bible Dictionary*, the name Athaliah means "afflicted of the Lord," and I define the name as "whom God afflicts." Athaliah actually murdered her own grandchildren to gain power (see 2 Chron. 22:11), outdoing the evil of her wicked mother. *Pulpit Commentary* writes:

> We find in this woman, Athaliah, the infernal tendencies of her father and her mother, Ahab and Jezebel. Though they had been swept as monsters from the earth, and were now lying in the grave, their hellish spirit lived and worked in this their daughter. It is, alas! often so. We have an immortality in others, as well as in ourselves. The men of long-forgotten generations still live in the present. Even the moral pulse of Adam throbs in all.

ATHALIAH'S UNLEASHING

Athaliah was the woman in the basket. And the angel pushed her back into the basket and closed the heavy lid again. The angel did this because it was not yet time for this spirit of Athaliah's ultimate uprising. While this spirit has been working in the earth, it is one of the satan's end-time secret weapons to wreak havoc on the church.

Few talk about Athaliah, and the few who do seem to scratch the surface of the depravity of this spirit or how to defeat it. I share more about this in my book *Jezebel's Revenge: Annihilating the Spirit of Athaliah*. I believe the dream revealed that the time of Athaliah's uprising is here. And most believers are unprepared to resist it. For that matter, most believers are not yet ready to accept the reality of the Jezebel spirit, much less this woman named Wickedness.

After the angel pushed Athaliah back into the basket, Zechariah's vision continued. He saw two women flying toward him, gliding on the wind. These were not angels because there are no female angels. Rather, these are a different form of spirit beings. These winged women came from heaven with wings filled with the wind. In Zechariah's vision, they took the basket and fly into the sky to Babylon to be set up on a pedestal. In my dream, they took the basket into the house. A temple is a house.

Could I have been in the temple built for Athaliah in my dream? Could it be possible that Athaliah is about to usurp Jezebel in the earth, exacting revenge on the prophets—and operating through some who are as ambitious and bloodthirsty as the Israelite queen we see pictured in the Bible? Could it be possible that the Jezebelic prophets will being following this greater evil? I believe some already are.

PROPHECY: A PURIFYING FIRE

I heard the Lord say:

A purifying fire is coming to the prophetic ministry—a baptism of fire is coming for those who will embrace it and let My fire do its perfect work. Those who resist the fire will be sidelined in the next season. Those who embrace My fire will be led into new realms of prophetic revelation and new levels of accuracy in the Spirit.

Those who understand the purifying work of My fire— the work of My fire to judge sin in your heart and refine you—will enter in willingly. They will walk into the fire freely, knowing that they are coming closer to My heart in the process. I am bringing My fire to the church. Embrace My fire. Don't resist My purifying work in your heart. I have great things stored up for you in the days ahead, but the path is for those holy hearts to walk on.

NOTE

1. Meredith G. Kline, *Glory in Our Midst* (Two-Age Press, 2001), 188.

CHAPTER 13

COMMISSIONING

A NEW GENERATION OF GENERALS

Just like there are seats on natural boards that govern the operations of corporations and churches alike, there are seats of governing authority in the spiritual realm. When those seats are left empty, the enemy works to fill the void.

Many generals of the faith have gone home to be with the Lord during my walk with God. Kenneth Hagin, Lester Sumrall, Derek Prince, T.L. Lowery, John Osteen, Steve Hill, Myles Munroe, John L. Sandford, C. Peter Wagner, John Paul Jackson, Kim Clement, Bob Jones, Paul Cain, and Billy Graham are just a few of the most notable who passed on to glory. As of the time of this writing, we have yet to see the uprising of a new generation that steps into the seats of governing authority these generals left empty.

Satan loves to fill a void. We know the enemy looks to fill voids, gaps, and vacuums. Luke 11:24-26 makes this painfully clear:

When an unclean spirit goes out of a man, he goes through dry places, seeking rest; and finding none, he says, "I will return to my house from which I came." And when he comes, he finds it swept and put in order. Then he goes and takes with him seven other spirits more wicked than himself, and they enter and dwell there; and the last state of that man is worse than the first.

You might ask, "How can being swept and put in order be a bad thing?" It's not bad, but it leaves a gap in the spirit. Just as we pray for a fresh baptism of the Holy Spirit after people are delivered, we need to stand in the gap as intercessors until the empty seat of governing authority is filled. Now is the time for intercessors to build a wall around the voids and fill the vacuums with the incense of prayer until God finds one, like Isaiah, who will say, "Here I am, Lord, send me" (see Isa. 6:8).

Remember, in my vision I heard the Lord say, "We need to assign new generals of war in this season because some have gone on to glory." I saw Jesus anointing and commissioning what I could best describe in natural terms as generals, captains, and sergeants. Jesus put His sword on the right shoulder of each officer in a commissioning ceremony. These generals were assigned to rally together captains and corporals and sergeants to wage warfare under the command of the Lord Jesus Christ.

A CHANGING OF THE GUARD

I remember the first time I visited Buckingham Palace and witnessed the changing of the guard, a formal ceremony in which the red-and-black-clad sentinels who guard the gates of the palace hand the baton to a new batch of watchmen. Accompanied by music, this elaborate ceremony takes about 45 minutes.

As major voices in the Body of Christ go home to be with the Lord, we can lean into the promises they carried for their generation. John 12:24 gives us faith to believe that the assignment of great men and women who ascended to glory can continue through those to whom they imparted. John 12:24 reads, "Most assuredly, I say to you, unless a grain of wheat falls into the ground and dies, it remains alone; but if it dies, it produces much grain."

James Goll, founder of God Encounters Ministries, points to the prophetic promises God gave to five seer prophets who are now in heaven—Bob Jones, John Paul Jackson, Kim Clement, John Sandford, and Paul Cain.

> Bob Jones released the prophetic promise of a Last Days "Billion Soul Harvest" especially among the youth of the earth. Papa Bob also challenged us with the piercing statement, "Did you learn to love?"
>
> John Paul Jackson labored for greater purity in the prophetic stream and a depth of accountability for the words spoken by the clay lips of revelatory vessels. John Paul was a true seer of seers and was noted for his precise predictions of the coming "Perfect Storm."
>
> Kim Clement was a musical seer like King David in the Bible. He contended for new creative inventions to release Kingdom wealth and that Jerusalem would be a united city in the midst of a time of great chaos. Often

Kim's highly potent prophetic nuggets were somewhat veiled and required the skill to dig for the hidden gold of the promise of God.

John Sandford was noted for his expertise in uniting the prophetic with counseling, inner healing and deliverance. He composed the landmark book, *The Elijah Task*. ...[He] contended for wholeness among the prophetic community and modeled honor to the First Nations people as a needed tool to "Heal the Land."

Paul Cain prophesied the "New Breed of a Nameless and Faceless Generation" who would only lift up the name of the One Man Christ Jesus. ...He declared with ferocity that the "Stadiums will be filled with a New Move of the Holy Spirit with Signs and Wonders."[1]

Goll asks a key question: "Are we in a Kairos time where the mantles of the prophetic and evangelism are converging? As this changing of the guard occurs, are we properly postured to inherit the revelatory promises released by these forerunners?"[2] He says, "Yes and amen!" and I agree. But who will respond to the call in the seer realms?

ANOINTING YOUNG WARRIOR APOSTLES

Paul the apostle was a warrior. He left us with Holy Spirit-inspired revelation on the hierarchy of satan's kingdom in Ephesians 6—and he endured plenty of warfare in his own right. He wrestled the beast of Ephesus (see 1 Cor. 15:32) and shook off a demonic attack on the

Isle of Malta (see Acts 28:5). He even dealt with a thorn in his side, a messenger of satan (see 2 Cor. 12:7).

Paul poured his life out as a drink offering in his generation and invested his heart into his spiritual son Timothy. Paul met the young man, who came from a mixed racial background, on his second missionary journey. Paul said of him, "I have no one like-minded, who will sincerely care for your state. For all seek their own, not the things which are of Christ Jesus. But you know his proven character, that as a son with his father he served with me in the gospel" (Phil. 2:20-22).

Paul commissioned Timothy by the laying on of hands, as referenced in Second Timothy 1:6-7, "Therefore I remind you to stir up the gift of God which is in you through the laying on of my hands. For God has not given us a spirit of fear, but of power and of love and of a sound mind." In First Timothy 1:18-19, we see Paul reminding his son of the commissioning:

> *This charge I commit to you, son Timothy, according to the prophecies previously made concerning you, that by them you may wage the good warfare, having faith and a good conscience, which some having rejected, concerning the faith have suffered shipwreck.*

Paul sent Timothy—whose name means "honoring God"—to check up on various churches he planted. Timothy practiced what Paul preached. Paul imparted a spiritual gift to him to establish him in his calling and continued training him until he ascended to glory. Paul and Timothy were co-laborers with each other and Christ. God is anointing young warrior apostles now to run with the generals of war before they go home to be with the Lord.

ANOINTING PROPHETIC WARRIORS

Prophets stir the pot because they release the voice of God into situations. The enemy, particularly Jezebel, hates the voice of God. God is anointing hearing ears, seeing eyes, and speaking mouths to hear, see, and say. God is raising up prophets, seers, and those with a heart to decree and declare God's will among the nations. Many will receive a double-portion anointing for the war ahead.

Consider Elisha's calling at the hand of Elijah. The transition of power wasn't immediate. It took time, but as Elisha served and pursued, he stepped into greater works.

> *"Elisha the son of Shaphat of Abel Meholah you shall anoint as prophet in your place. It shall be that whoever escapes the sword of Hazael, Jehu will kill; and whoever escapes the sword of Jehu, Elisha will kill. Yet I have reserved seven thousand in Israel, all whose knees have not bowed to Baal, and every mouth that has not kissed him."*
>
> *So he departed from there, and found Elisha the son of Shaphat, who was plowing with twelve yoke of oxen before him, and he was with the twelfth. Then Elijah passed by him and threw his mantle on him. And he left the oxen and ran after Elijah, and said, "Please let me kiss my father and my mother, and then I will follow you."*

And he said to him, "Go back again, for what have I done to you?"

So Elisha turned back from him, and took a yoke of oxen and slaughtered them and boiled their flesh, using the oxen's equipment, and gave it to the people, and they ate. Then he arose and followed Elijah, and became his servant (1 Kings 19:16-21).

God anointed this young man to pick up where Elijah left off. God will anoint prophetic warriors who possess humility and faithfulness—and who are surrendered to the call. He is anointing those who refuse to look back or seek to get ahead of the process. He will cause them to speak with authority and not as the religious scribes (see Mark 1:22). They will do miracles and remain loyal to the purposes of God.

ANOINTING NEW WARRING KINGS

Indeed, changing of the guard is underway. God wants to anoint new worshiping warriors to lead us on to the next battlefields like David. King Saul was the first king of Israel. His heart strayed from the Lord and he lost his kingship. This grieved Samuel, who had invested plenty into Saul.

Yet a changing of the guard occurred in the spirit before it ever occurred in the natural. The Lord told Samuel to fill his horn with oil and go to the house of Jesse in Bethlehem to anoint a king from among his sons. Samuel invited Jesse and his sons to a sacrifice and prepared to initiate the spiritual transition. We read the account in First Samuel 16:6-13:

> So it was, when they came, that he looked at Eliab and said, "Surely the Lord's anointed is before Him!" But the Lord said to Samuel, "Do not look at his appearance or at his physical stature, because I have refused him. For the Lord does not see as man sees; for man looks at the outward appearance, but the Lord looks at the heart."
>
> So Jesse called Abinadab, and made him pass before Samuel. And he said, "Neither has the Lord chosen this one." Then Jesse made Shammah pass by. And he said, "Neither has the Lord chosen this one." Thus Jesse made seven of his sons pass before Samuel. And Samuel said to Jesse, "The Lord has not chosen these." And Samuel said to Jesse, "Are all the young men here?" Then he said, "There remains yet the youngest, and there he is, keeping the sheep."
>
> And Samuel said to Jesse, "Send and bring him. For we will not sit down till he comes here." So he sent and brought him in. Now he was ruddy, with bright eyes, and good-looking. And the Lord said, "Arise, anoint him; for this is the one!" Then Samuel took the horn of oil and anointed him in the midst of his brothers; and the Spirit of the Lord came upon David from that day forward.

Samuel was a seer charged with anointing a worshiping-warrior king. But natural eyes fooled him at the start. Samuel was sure Eliab, the eldest, was God's choice because of the birthright and his appearance. God is not choosing new generation generals based on birthright or appearance. He is looking at the heart. The future generals who arise may surprise many of us.

A NEW BREED OF DELIVERANCE MINISTERS

We will also see a new breed of deliverance ministers rise. Derek Prince is a legend in deliverance ministry. The Lord spoke to me:

> *I am raising up even now, in your midst, a new generation and a new breed of deliverance ministers. And they will be bold like lions. They will not shrink back nor will they be intimidated by the tactics of the enemy. For I am putting new mantles on My deliverance ministers who are willing to take the tough cases, who are willing to go where others will not venture.*
>
> *And I am going to give them new revelations and new flows of My anointing. New rivers will flow out of them as I pour My anointing into them. And they will see even clearly inside bodies what is going on, where the stronghold is. They will see the names of the demons even written in the spirit, like the handwriting that was written on the wall in the days of Daniel.*
>
> *And they will cooperate one with another; they will become companies of deliverance ministers who will run together. They will share intelligence, and they will*

cooperate with one another for My glory. For there will not be a strong competition in the realm of deliverance as we see even now in the realm of the apostolic and in the realm of the prophetic, because these ministers have set themselves apart and they understand the need for clean hands and a pure heart.

So they will celebrate with one another and celebrate each other and they will relish the victories over the kingdom of darkness together. And they will network together, not in the sense of building their own kingdom, but in order to share the stories of glory from My Spirit in the realm of deliverance.

I am doing a new thing in deliverance ministry. Have you not yet heard about it? Well, I am announcing it to you even now in a bold way. Begin to watch and begin to pray. But also, know and recognize that many will come and try to take this new mantle—this new time and season of deliverance ministers rising up—as a fad and a trend. And they will try to hook their wagon to the greater wagon and try to use the momentum of the tide and the flow that I am bringing to the Body of Christ.

But they will not carry the authority because their heart is compromised. They will not carry the authority that the pure ones do because they are not in it for the right reasons, and they will end up like the sons of

> *Sceva because I don't know these ones—not the way that I need to know them—because they kept part of their heart back from Me. And watch as the false deliverers arise, needing deliverance themselves. And you will see and know that I will sweep through the Body of Christ and I will do a new thing in deliverance ministry in this hour.*

WHAT WE WILL SEE NEXT

Prophetically speaking, we are going to see the rise of unlikely generals in the years ahead. These leaders have been hidden in the wilderness like John the Baptist. They carry a purity of heart and a bold word in their mouth that will stir and even topple some religious systems. Jezebel will rise up and resist those who carry the spirit of Elijah, but Jehus will manifest in tandem to throw her down.

While men have dominated the highest rankings in the army of God, more women will rise up to take their seats at the table in God's boardroom. Deborahs will arise where Baraks wouldn't answer the call. We will also see younger generals take their positions, like Joshua and Gideon, as God accelerates the timetables. We will see strategic partnerships between the Joshuas and Calebs—the young and the old—who demonstrate mutual respect and overwhelming victories.

We will see supernatural soldiers who understand the dynamics of the spirit realm, including the heavenly host that harkens to the voice of God's Word (see Ps. 103). Remember, as Jesus was commissioning these generals of war, I saw angels standing right behind each one He was commissioning. It looked almost like catchers in a church who stand behind those who are receiving the laying on of hands in response to an altar call. However, I believe these were warring angels assigned to the generals to help them in battle. The angels' shadows almost seemed to clothe them and fell in front of them. That's how closely the warring angels assigned to these generals will walk with them.

NOTES

1. James W. Goll, "Changing of the Guard: The Convergence of Prophecy and Evangelism," God Encounters Ministries, What Promises Are We to Inherit? March 11, 2019, https://godencounters.com/changing-of-the-guard.

2. Ibid.

CHAPTER 14

THE MYSTERY

OF UNITY IN WARFARE

I saw a vast army rising up in a triangular formation with one leading the charge and ranks spreading out line by line behind them. I had no knowledge of this, but this configuration is a warfare strategy dating back to the days of the ancient Greeks and Romans. It's called the wedge formation. Alexander the Great used the wedge formation against the Persian cavalry because its narrow point pierces enemy lines with a concentration of power at the front.

Prophetically speaking, one thing strikes me about this formation: There is a clear leader and everyone else is following that leader in lockstep. In recent decades, we've seen that everyone wants to be number one but fewer are willing to be number two and three, which are equally vital. Fewer want to be among the masses in the army, which are critical to the overall success of the battle plan.

As we begin to grasp the mystery of unity in warfare, we will appreciate there can only be one leader—and that leader is Jesus. As soldiers in the army of God, we must pledge our allegiance to Jesus, the Captain of the Hosts. When we are one with Him in the secret place, we will be one with Him on the battlefield no matter what human leader is at the head of the wedge formation. This is the part of the mystery of unity in spiritual warfare.

Jesus spoke of the prayer of agreement in Matthew 18. From the principle in this passage, we understand unity brings God's Kingdom and will to earth through prayer. In Matthew 18:18-20, Jesus offered these words on unified prayer in the context of spiritual warfare:

> *Truly I tell you, whatever you forbid and declare to be improper and unlawful on earth must be what is already forbidden in heaven, and whatever you permit and declare proper and lawful on earth must be what is already permitted in heaven. Again I tell you, if two of you on earth agree (harmonize together, make a symphony together) about whatever [anything and everything] they may ask, it will come to pass and be done for them by My Father in heaven. For wherever two or three are gathered (drawn together as My followers) in (into) My name, there I Am in the midst of them* (AMPC).

DEMYSTIFYING UNITY

You've heard it said one can put a thousand to flight and two can put ten thousand to flight. That is only true if there is unity between the two. Without unity, the believer would do better warring against the one thousand alone and cooperating with angels as backup. Angels are always in unity with God's Word. The unity between the two Matthew 18 describes releases a frequency that guarantees answers.

Unity—this harmony, this symphony—is truly music to God's ears. When He hears unity, I believe He surrounds us with songs of deliverance from our enemies (see Ps. 32:7). Where there is unity between men—and between men and God's purposes and plans—God commands a blessing (see Ps. 133). *The Passion Translation* of Psalm 133 really draws this out this harmony:

> *How truly wonderful and delightful to see brothers and sisters living together in sweet unity! It's as precious as the sacred scented oil flowing from the head of the high priest Aaron, dripping down upon his beard and running all the way down to the hem of his priestly robes.*
>
> *This heavenly harmony can be compared to the dew dripping down from the skies upon Mount Hermon, refreshing the mountain slopes of Israel. For from this realm of sweet harmony God will release his eternal blessing, the promise of life forever!*

Where God's blessing rests, the enemy's curse cannot land. Part of the blessing—like the oil poured on Aaron's head that flowed down to his beard—is the anointing that breaks the yoke of the enemy (see Isa. 10:27). *Pulpit Commentary* adds this helpful note: "Here one man's infirmity is upheld by another's strength; one man's short-sightedness compensated by another's wider view; this man's little faith overpowered by that man's firm confidence."

The mystery of unity in warfare is the pure, selfless, God-inspired agreement that draws heaven's resources to earth to thwart the plans and purposes of the enemy who opposes us at every turn.

TURNING TOGETHER ON A DIME

The army of God has always had every advantage over the enemy until sin or strife entered the camp. Achan's sin caused the Israelite army to lose a battle. In Joshua 6:18-19, God said:

> And you, by all means abstain from the accursed things, lest you become accursed when you take of the accursed things, and make the camp of Israel a curse, and trouble it. But all the silver and gold, and vessels of bronze and iron, are consecrated to the Lord; they shall come into the treasury of the Lord.

The entire army of God was unified under Joshua's leadership—except Achan. Achan was not in harmony with God. He took a garment and some silver and gold from the enemy's camp, and this breach of unity cost the lives of many.

Strife also gives the enemy an advantage over us. Strife intrudes on the harmony. One definition of strife is "bitter, sometimes violent conflict or dissension; an act of contention." James 3:16 warns us, "For where envying and strife is, there is confusion and every evil work" (KJV). We can't send confusion into the enemy's camp when there's confusion of this nature in our camps. There is no unity in the enemy's camp. His kingdom won't stand because it's divided against itself (see Matt. 3:24). Unity remains a mysterious Kingdom strategy that too few are considering. The wedge formation demands unity to achieve victory.

Part of the power of a wedge formation is nimbleness. In the wedge, the military unit is light-footed in the spirit. The troops can turn quickly. In the vision, I saw a prophetic people who hear the Lord so freely they are able to turn on a dime. I saw a trust forming between generals and the ranks. A unity in which no soldier breaks rank, claiming, "The Holy Spirit told me." This is a unity with the Captain of the Hosts running so deep that when one solider hears the command, the rest are hearing the same thing. There's no question about strategy or tactics because everybody is hearing the same thing.

This new warfare requires companies of soldiers to come together under the banner of Christ with great trust—those who understand order and authority. It's as if this new-breed army is receiving its marching orders straight from the war room in heaven and the charge of the leader is merely confirmation, so everyone immediately agrees. There is no debate, no time wasted, no defectors, none AWOL. That's what it's going to take to win the battles in the end times. It's not man's strategies; it's heaven's strategies. Experience alone will not win the fight, but heaven's blueprints will map the way to victory.

THE DANGER OF BREAKING RANKS

In this epic battle to come, we need all the spiritual warriors in formation. But the Holy Spirit has shown me that some have broken rank in the past and need to come back to the battle line. In a military sense, ranks are the members of an armed service—the enlisted personnel, not the officers. Breaking ranks is disobeying the orders of the commander. Breaking ranks is to publicly disagree with your battalion. Breaking ranks is to move out of the wedge. I heard the Lord say:

> *Many are breaking rank. They are sitting on the sidelines when they should be waging warfare. Some of them were wounded in battle. Some of them were even hit with friendly fire. They are tending to their wounds and they are out of formation. When they hear this message about new weapons for a new season—about spiritual warfare technologies—their spirit will bear witness. They will get a new revelation that will bring healing and strengthen them for the battle. They will pick up their weapons and run to the battle line—and they will even call others forth who have been hanging back.*

Now, I don't believe the Holy Spirit was talking about those who are compromising the gospel, the hyper-grace adherents, the gay-affirming theologians and the rest. Yes, they are breaking ranks. But it goes beyond this. I believe He was speaking specifically about those spiritual warriors who have withdrawn from battle—they have broken ranks.

Naturally speaking, in some cases, the ranks have been wounded by the officers leading them, sending them into a battle they weren't trained well enough to fight or throwing them in the line of fire to protect themselves. In other cases, ranks have wounded themselves by not following orders or been hit with friendly fire from others in

God's army who were careless or disobedient. Whatever the case, it's time to get back into formation. David's mighty men did not break rank. Gideon's army did not break rank. As soldiers in the army of the Lord, we must not break rank. We must remain loyal to the Captain of the Hosts.

If you've been wounded by friendly fire in battle, forgive those who hurt you and let the Lord heal you so you can take your rightful place. God needs you on your post. You have a place in the triangular formation I saw in the spirit.

If you've been oppressed by the enemy and are fearful of returning to the front lines, take counsel with wise warriors who can take authority in prayer over the enemy's assignment against your life, help you discover new spiritual warfare technologies, and stand with you in warfare. God needs you on your post. If you've rebelled against God, repent, receive forgiveness, and pick up your weapons again. You don't disengage from the war just because you choose not to fight. The battle against you will continue to rage. Get back in formation. God needs you on your post.

A PROPHETIC WARNING TO WARRIORS

I heard the Lord say:

> *Mark those among you who cause division. Beware of those who sow seeds of discord. These acts of spiritual violence breed witchcraft and pain. Choose to walk in*

such a level of peace and in such an alert spirit that you quickly discern dividers, detractors, and distractors who pull you out of My presence and My will. Pluck up the seeds of discord that have been sown in your soul. Slam the door on gossip and slander. Repent of agreeing with the accuser of the brethren and bless those who have cursed you.

I have called you not to fight every battle alone. I've called you to stand with others. For one can put 1,000 to flight and two can put 10,000 to flight and together you will see swift victory. Stubborn battles that could not seem to be won will be won in an instant as you stand together in unity. For where there is unity, I command a blessing. That blessing is called victory, increase, retribution, and vindication. By allowing Me to use you as a war club for your brothers and sisters, I will bring increase to you and the spoils of war will be part and parcel of your reward.

CHAPTER 15

THE MYSTERY
OF GOD'S WORLD WAR III

I saw a vision of the war room in heaven. I believe that war room has always existed. After all, there was once a war in heaven. But what I saw in the war room was something more than preparation for an average war.

Remember, angels and saints were sitting at the table. Jehovah Gibbor was outlining a strategy. Our mighty God was preparing an army for battle, handing out assignments and commissioning new generals. This was not just another war. I believe God is planning for a spiritual World War III that Bishop Hamon prophesied about.

> The word I am sharing from Christ's letter to the Philadelphia church, of us being granted an open door that no man or demon can shut, is directed mainly to those who have ears to hear what Christ is saying to His church, who are walking in all presently restored truth

and have volunteered to be warriors in God's newly acti-vated, offensive and powerful army called God's World War 3.[1]

Hamon points to Psalm 110:3, which says "Your people will vol-unteer freely in the day of Your power" (NASB) or "Your troops will be willing on your day of battle" (NIV). Hamon says God is searching for soldiers of the cross who are willing to volunteer for God's World War III offensive army.

> Jesus is looking for those who have level-four heart soil (Matt. 13:23), which has been purged from all weed-seed attitudes. They are righteous and fearless, for they have attained to level three of the overcomers—"they loved not their lives unto the death" (Rev. 12:11b).
>
> God is going to give them His mighty strength…. Jesus, as commander in chief of His army, is coming to put His mighty warrior anointing upon them to destroy the powers of darkness and demonstrate God's kingdom throughout the earth.[2]

PROPHETIC WARNINGS OF WORLD WAR

Hamon's use of world war terminology is purposeful. There's plenty of talk about a natural World War III in news headlines. It seems threats are coming from China, Iran, Russia, North Korea, and beyond. Secular newspaper headlines are littered with doomsday the-ories about the end of the world in the wake of a nuclear attack.

What we see in the natural is a manifestation of what is going on in the spirit realm—where the real war is. Clearly, God's World War III is brewing in the spirit realm and He will reign victorious. He's never lost a battle and He never will. God is looking for prayer warriors to stand in the gap and push back darkness—with generals leading the way.

When Jesus' disciples asked Him about the end of the age and the sign of His coming, His answer was clear:

> *Take heed that no one deceives you. For many will come in My name, saying, "I am the Christ," and will deceive many. And you will hear of wars and rumors of wars. See that you are not troubled; for all these things must come to pass, but the end is not yet. For nation will rise against nation, and kingdom against kingdom. And there will be famines, pestilences, and earthquakes in various places. All these are the beginning of sorrows* (Matthew 24:4-8).

When Holy Spirit shares with His prophets and seers words, dreams, visions, and encounters of war, we should not be troubled. This is all part of Jehovah Gibbor's master plan, and it's merely the beginning of sorrows. With so many prophetic warnings of war, death, pestilence, plague, and destruction, the signs of the times would point to the beginning of sorrows as a now reality. I've had a few of these encounters myself.

Travail Over China Invading Taiwan

Leaving Taiwan in 2018 in a wheelchair due to a severe sprained ankle, what felt like deep sorrow engulfed me. I waxed silent and then began to gently weep as I was wheeled through the airport. I was speechless, caught in a vision that I could not escape even though I didn't want to see it.

The Lord showed me the enemy's plans for death and destruction in Taiwan. I saw an army from mainland China invading the land in effort to bring Taiwan fully back into the communist fold. It shook me to the point that I could not even speak when asked what the matter was. I could not shake the images of the army marching, the resistance from Taiwan, and the bloodshed. We continue to pray.

A Vision of a Nuclear Attack on Manhattan

It was a sudden encounter with visionary revelation that must be shared—and spur the intercessors to stand in the gap. I was traveling from Awakening House of Prayer D.C. to Awakening House of Prayer New York City on a train. When we disembarked at Penn Station, I saw a sign that said "Fire Storm." The sign caught my attention like the burning bush caught Moses' attention, and I was suddenly caught up in a vision.

In this vision, I saw New York City engulfed in what I can best describe as nuclear snow. I saw people running frantically through the streets in terror. Like a camera zooming in for emphasis, I saw a small child with his hands over his ears screaming. In a word, it was chaos.

When I asked the Lord who was launching these attacks, I saw a room filled with military officers. Like a camera panning upward, I saw the shoes of one man, then the pants, jacket, and collar. The uniform was brown and the collar was red. Just then, I was interrupted and did not see their faces but feel confident more than one nation was represented in the room.

Unmistakably, the uniform was North Korean. Although North Korea doesn't have the missile technology to hit Manhattan yet, some weapons analysts argue North Korea could potentially hit New York in the future depending on the trajectory of the launch. In a partnership with Russia, this could happen.

What I saw next confirmed the threat carries greater urgency: North Korea is in bed with Russia. I began researching legitimate ties between these two countries and what could cause them to work together at this moment in history. Immediately, I discovered the history of North Korea initiated at the end of World War II in 1945. When Japan surrendered, Korea was divided at the 38th parallel.

The Soviet Union occupied the north and the United States occupied the south. These superpowers could not come to terms with unifying the country so two individual governments were formed. The People's Republic of Korea (or North Korea) aligned with the Soviet Union. The Republic of Korea (or South Korea) aligned with the West.

In other words, Russia has had historic ties with communist Korea since its founding. With this, the dots are starting to connect. In 2003, the Lord told me, "Don't trust the bear." I didn't know what that meant when I first heard it, but the bear is the symbol for Russia.

With the help of the Russians, North Korea—and most likely China—is planning a nuclear attack on New York City—and not just New York City but a coordinated attack on other strategic cities in America. These plans will collapse as intercessors stand in the gap.

This is not the judgment of God on America but an enemy plan to steal, kill, and destroy (see John 10:10).

Kim Clement's Prophecies of the "Beast of the East"

In 2010, the late prophet Kim Clement prophesied a war in Europe, with a focus on France. Although there was plenty of tension as Great Britain exited the European Union, there was nothing near a war. But intercessors should keep their eyes open. Clement prophesied:

> There was a war in the heavenlies with the Prince of Persia. There was a battle going on, as there is today. ...A war will take place. It shall be short-lived because, as France destroyed the power of invasion from the Middle East in the 7th century, so shall they rise up and destroy the invading forces of the beast of the east. ...There will be a second reformation in Europe. God says, "I will begin in France. All the tribes of the earth will be affected by the sound."[3]

Cindy Jacobs Prophesies Potential World War

In 2019, Cindy Jacobs, co-founder of Generals International, released a prophetic warning that there would be a problem with Iran that could escalate into World War III—and that we needed to pray about it. This manifested when Iran's General Soleimani was taken out by the U.S. government. Cindy rallied intercessors and the crisis was averted, but it took us one step closer to an eventual World War III.

We know the enemy works to change times and laws (see Dan. 7:25). The Holy Spirit told me the time for a natural World War III is not yet. All eyes are on Israel, which is where a likely conflict leading to World War III could center on. In 2019, I heard the Lord say:

> *My purposes will not be thwarted. My will shall be done and My Kingdom shall come to the earth, and sooner than many people think. I am asking you to lift up your voices and pray in the face of the wars and rumors of wars. For the time is not yet for the escalation the enemy has planned.*
>
> *Take authority now with your voice. Open your lips and cry aloud by the power of My Spirit. Release your decrees and give ammunition to the angel armies. Take a stand and fight for what is right in the Spirit. I will move speedily to shut down the work of the enemy that has some men's hearts failing them because of fear. You do your part and I will do my part. Pray.*

Rick Joyner Prophesies New Civil War

In 2018, I saw a new civil war coming to America. Rick Joyner, founder of MorningStar Ministries, also had a dream in December 2018 about various attacks coming on the United States. In the dream, he says he was waiting in line to fight when an angel approached him about a different assignment.

I was then taken to a large device that was showing "A History of The American Republic from Heaven's Perspective." As I watched this, I saw that if I walked across the face of this device, to my right the times progressed toward the present. I decided to go to the end to see heaven's perspective on what was happening now. When I came to the present, there was a sentence written in brilliant glowing golden letters: "The Second American Revolutionary/ Civil War is inevitable, it is right, and it will be successful."[4]

We can see a civil war, of sorts, playing out before our eyes as various ideologies battle for dominance while the oppressed battle for liberty. Joyner writes:

There will be champions raised up that will go out to attack the specific evil strongholds in our nation. These evils were things like bigotry, greed, selfish ambition, hatred, rebellion, pride, etc. In the dream, all of these evils were in trees, which speaks of them having roots and branches. To defeat them, one must not waste time flailing at the branches, but rather put an ax to the root of the tree.[5]

NOTES

1. Bill Hamon, "Prophetic Word: Preparing for God's World War 3," Charisma Magazine, 2016, https://www.charismamag.com/

blogs/prophetic-insight/28488-prophetic-word-preparing-for -god-s-world-war-3.

2. Ibid.

3. Kim Clement, "France Will Rise Up to Destroy the Beast of the East," Paris, France, November, 2010, https://youtu.be/ wkaxS4OB3cw.

4. Rick Joyner, "The Second American Revolutionary/Civil War," MorningStar Ministries, January 1, 2019, https://publications .morningstarministries.org/resources/word-week/2019/second -american-revolutionarycivil-war.

5. Rick Joyner, "The Second American Revolutionary/Civil War, Part 2," MorningStar Ministries, January 4, 2019, https:// publications.morningstarministries.org/resources/word -week/2019/second-american-revolutionarycivil-war-part-2.

and educational systems because of a misapplied interpretation of the phrase, "separation of church and state." We must see a shift in this arena in order to preserve the Christian heritage that America was founded upon. The goal is to put in place righteous political leaders that will positively affect all aspects of government.

The Mountain of Media

The media mountain includes news sources such as radio, TV news stations, newspapers, Internet news and opinion (blog) sites and etc. The media has the potential to sway popular opinion on current issues based upon its reporting, which is not always truthful or accurate. In the 2008 elections, the liberal "elite" media played a vital role, especially in the Presidential race. Their generally supportive and positive reporting greatly influenced the outcome.

There has been a rise in Christian news services, which is needed. However, to bring transformation to the mountain of media, Christians who are gifted for and called into this type of work must be willing to report righteously and truthfully in the secular marketplace.

The Mountain of Arts and Entertainment

In this mountain we find some of the most influential forces shaping our society. Music, filmmaking, television, social media, and the performing arts drive the cultural tastes, values and standards of a nation's citizens, particularly its youth.

With a heavy reliance on the strong appeal of sex, drugs and alcohol, the arts and entertainment industries wield significant influence. The body of Christ needs powerful, righteous men and women who are not afraid to take their God-given talent into the arts and entertainment arenas. People ready to further His purposes, while impacting those who are lost in darkness and would not otherwise be interested in any kind of Christian message in traditional forms.

The Mountain of Business

The ability to literally create wealth through ingenuity, enterprise, creativity and effort and is a God-given gift and a universal impulse. The markets and economic systems that emerge whenever people are free to pursue buying and selling become the lifeblood of a nation. This includes anything from farms to small businesses to large corporations.

Of course this realm is prone to corruption through idolatry, greed and covetousness. In response, the Church must embrace its responsibility to train up those who are called into the marketplace to manage businesses and provide leadership with integrity and honesty. We believe it is the Lord's will to make His people prosperous and that He desires for His Church to use its wealth to finance the work of Kingdom expansion. Simply put: Prosperity with a purpose.[1]

NOTE

1. Generals International, "The Seven Mountains of Societal Influence," accessed October 20, 2020, https://www.generals .org/the-seven-mountains.

CHAPTER 17

A GLIMPSE

INTO SATAN'S WAR ROOM

The enemy counterfeits the Kingdom, so we know satan's kingdom has a war room. That's a sobering thought. Just like God's war room in heaven, satan's war room is in the unseen realm. Satan's war room is not in hell—he's not there yet. Hell's everlasting fire was created for the devil and his angels (see Matt. 25:41). But he's not there yet. No, hell is not satan's home—it's his ultimate place of judgment. Satan's war room is right here on the earth.

When God cast lucifer, who later became satan, out of heaven with one-third of the angels, he landed on the earth that God created. Remember, Jesus said He saw satan fall like lightning from heaven (see Luke 10:18). And Revelation 12:9 tells us, "So the great dragon was cast out, that serpent of old, called the Devil and Satan, who deceives the whole world; he was cast to the earth, and his angels were cast out with him."

During Christ's temptation, we get more insight into satan's rulership. In Matthew 4:8-9 we read, "Again, the devil took Him up on an exceedingly high mountain, and showed Him all the kingdoms of the world and their glory. And he said to Him, 'All these things I will give You if You will fall down and worship me.'" The Bible called it a temptation. It would not have been a temptation if satan didn't have the power to give Jesus what was promised.

Adam sold the lease on earth to satan when he sinned, eating from the fruit of the tree of the knowledge of good and evil. In that moment, satan became the ruler of this world. Therefore, satan had the power to give the world to Jesus. Jesus called him the ruler of this world several times (see John 14:30; 12:31; 16:11). The ruler, or prince, of the world was the rabbinic title for satan.

THE PRINCE OF THE POWER OF THE AIR

What does that mean, exactly? The Greek word for *ruler* in this verse is *archon*. It means ruler, commander, chief, and leader, according to *The KJV New Testament Greek Lexicon*. Strong's Concordance adds "a first (in rank or power): chief (ruler), magistrate, prince." Paul called him the prince of the power of the air (see Eph. 2:2). A ruler is one who rules—or one who sets laws, regulations, procedures, customs and habits, principles, standards, and judgments.

Before the Book of Genesis was penned, Job gave us insight into satan's activity in the earth. There was a time when satan approached the throne of God: "And the Lord said to Satan, 'From where do you come?' So Satan answered the Lord and said, 'From going to and fro on the earth, and from walking back and forth on it'" (Job 1:7). Peter understood satan was still doing the same: "your adversary the devil walks about like a roaring lion, seeking whom he may devour" (1 Pet. 5:8.)

John said the whole world is under the sway of the wicked one (see 1 John 5:19). As Christians, we are not under satan's rulership. We are in the world but not of the world (see John 15:19). Jesus is our Ruler. At the end of this age, when the seventh angel sounds, we will hear loud voices in heaven saying, "The kingdoms of this world have become the kingdoms of our Lord and of His Christ, and He shall reign forever and ever!" (Rev. 11:15).

Speaking of the Revelation war in heaven, *Barnes' Notes on the Bible* says, "What weapons Satan may use to destroy the church, and in what way his efforts may be counteracted by holy angels, are points on which we can have little knowledge. It is sufficient to know that the fact of such a struggle is not improbable, and that Satan is successfully resisted by the leader of the heavenly host." Until then, satan is strategizing against the saints in his war room on earth.

THE DEVIL'S DEVICES

Paul tells us plainly in Second Corinthians 2:11 not to be ignorant of the devil's devices. *The Message* says, "we're not oblivious to his sly ways." The New Living Translation speaks of not letting satan outsmart us, "for we are familiar with his evil schemes." And *The Passion Translation* puts it this way: "so that we would not be exploited by the adversary, satan, for we know his clever schemes."

The Greek word for *ignorant* in that verse is *agnoeo*, which in this context means "to be ignorant, not to know; not to understand, unknown," according to *The KJV New Testament Greek Lexicon*. We must be a student of God and His Word, but God warns about the enemy's nature, character, and ploys—and gives us clear examples of his machinations against the saints—throughout Scripture. Clearly, God does want us to understand the enemy's devices.

SATAN STRATEGIZED AGAINST JOB

The enemy comes up with his schemes, plots, and plans in his war room on earth. Just as God gave Joshua, David, Gideon and others war strategies, satan gives his army war strategies. We know when satan was roaming the earth, he came up with a war strategy against Job. His first strategy was to accuse Job to God, attacking his character.

In his book, *Army of the Dawn, Part II*, Rick Joyner makes a profound statement that we must understand if we want to thwart the activities in satan's war room. "Scriptures reveal that two acts occur continually before the throne of God—intercession and accusation. The conflict between these two is a focal point of the battle between the Kingdom of God and the kingdom of darkness."[1] Indeed, one of the names for satan is the Accuser of the Brethren (see Rev. 12:10-11). Intercession disarms the weapon of accusation. Job needed intercessors. Job 1:9-12 gives us insight into this satanic weapon:

> *"Does Job fear God for nothing? Have You not made a hedge around him, around his household, and around all that he has on every side? You have blessed the work of his hands,*

and his possessions have increased in the land. But now, stretch out Your hand and touch all that he has, and he will surely curse You to Your face!" And the Lord said to Satan, "Behold, all that he has is in your power; only do not lay a hand on his person." So Satan went out from the presence of the Lord.

Satan used a phased approach to his attack on Job. His first strategy was to have raiders come in and steal his oxen and donkeys. Next, a fire burned up the sheep and servants. Then, raiders took away his camels and killed more of his servants. After that, a great wind struck the house where his children were having a party and they all died.

If that weren't enough, the devil influenced his wife to suggest he curse God and die and spurred his friends to criticize him when he was at his lowest point. The final tactic in the strategy was to come against Job's health. Can you see it? The enemy's strategy is not always the same, and it won't work on us if we strategize with the Holy Spirit. He sees every intricate detail of the enemy's plan.

A VISION OF SATAN'S WAR ROOM

I have never seen satan's war room, but the late Jill Austin, founder of Master Potter Ministries, did. She reported she had an open vision and saw a gambling casino covering the earth. She describes global players who were competing for control of the world's resources—gold, silver, oil, and water. Some nations considered genocide of an entire people group just to take over the gold mines in the land.

They were playing with cards—gambling and playing for high stakes. These players' faces were like dogs. They had thick collars on, with spikes, and they were smoking expensive cigars. They were laughing crudely, and they were drunk and drinking whiskey. The scene looked like one of the paintings by Coolidge, which shows dogs gambling like men. But then I saw Kingdom Players of the Lord—a Holy Mafia that came and sat at the table to play for world resources. They were undetected— they were the Lord's "007 agents" playing a very deadly and dangerous game.[2]

Here's where it gets especially interesting in the context of the war room discussion. Austin went into a war room with huge maps. She recalls the back wall of the war room was living, as was a picture of the world with all the nations. From this place, the families started making more evil plots.

They said, "Let's blow up three embassies. Let's have three old women go to the mall and blow themselves up. Let's have several university campuses bombed. Let's have mass shootings at two schools. Let's have trains and planes bombed." They began to orchestrate a world terror, with fear, death, war, and disease hitting the earth. The news media went crazy and the world moved in great fear. Then they said about the world, "They want peace at any price? So, they want a military police state?" And eventually this would move into one world government.[3]

Austin says these ancient families had strings attached to all the world leaders to become popes, kings, presidents, prime ministers, and the like. These families essentially bought the nations. The good news, she wrote, is the Lord is raising up an Enoch Company—a group of intercessors who will be translated into these secret evil alliances and hear the plans of satan, and then return to the councils of God to legislate "holy plans" to devour the evil plans of the enemy. Again, they were undetected—they were the Lord's "007 agents."

SATAN'S SLANDER WAR

In his 1973 book *The Vision*, David Wilkerson had a vision of satan's slander war. (The book is no longer in print.) In it, he was convinced satan has declared war on every true minister of Jesus Christ and will leave no stone unturned in attempts to discredit and shipwreck every person of God who is determined to stay true. He prophesied satan would raise up "gossip mongers" to harass, malign, and lie on them.

> Ministers who thought they had no enemies in the world will wake up to discover that someone is talking about them. Pastors of churches are going to face the most malicious gossip of all. Innuendos, lies, and false statements that will be floating around will come from the very pits of Hell.
>
> It will be a supernatural demonstration of demonic powers. Not a single true minister of the gospel will be immune. The wives of ministers who are married will also come under attack.

Legions of lying spirits have been turned loose upon the world with the single purpose of accusing Christians through gossip and slander. This gossip war will not only be aimed against ministers of the gospel but against all true believers of Jesus Christ, of all colors and creeds.[4]

SATAN'S MASTER POWER

Satan's master power is witchcraft. I'm not talking about the kind of witchcraft like you see on sitcoms or movies. I'm not talking about a witch riding a broom. I am talking about a supernatural force that principalities release. Just as the Holy Spirit is the power of God, witchcraft is the power of the enemy. It's been taught in past generations that the enemy's weapons are merely lies and deception. I disagree. Witchcraft is a master power.

The Word of God takes a strong stance against witchcraft because those who practice it are essentially bowing to satan himself and being used as a weapon of warfare in the earth. Deuteronomy 18:9-12 calls witchcraft an abomination. An abomination is something of extreme disgust and loathing, according to *Merriam-Webster*'s dictionary. God showed me in December 2019 He was going to begin to deal with abominations in the Body of Christ with a stronger hand.

Witchcraft provokes the Lord to anger (see 2 Kings 17:17). There's witchcraft in terms of divination, which the Lord hates. I wrote more about this in my book, *Discerning Prophetic Witchcraft*. There's witchcraft in terms of the Galatians 5 works of the flesh, which will keep people from inheriting the Kingdom of God. But there's another kind of witchcraft mentioned in the Bible—a weaponized witchcraft principalities release.

A REVIVAL OF THE DEVIL'S WITCHCRAFT

The great Voice of Healing, miracle-working evangelist A.A. Allen saw what was the beginning of a revival of the devil's witchcraft. That was back in the 1950s—before prayer was even taken out of schools. Now, witchcraft is a mega movement. The enemy is working to fascinate a generation with occult phenomenon. A.A. Allen's discernment was profound.

"An awful lot of people are sick, diseased and afflicted under a curse, under a spell because of the present revival of witchcraft around the world," Allen declared. "There has never been a time in history when there has been such a devil's revival of witchcraft."[5] That was true in Allen's day, but it's no longer true. The occult and witchcraft are more prevalent now than ever. Indeed, while many in the Body of Christ are contending for a Third Great Awakening, the enemy has already pulled of a great awakening to witchcraft and the occult.

In the end times, there will be a rise of occultism practices, including witchcraft and sorcery, because the enemy knows the punishment for these practices and is working to kill as many people as possible spiritually before the million-soul harvest Bob Jones prophesied. Revelation 18:23 says Babylon's sorcery deceived all nations. That's a big—but true—statement. Revelation 21:8 says sorcerers will burn in lake of fire and sulfur, which is the second death.

Indeed, we're seeing a revival of the devil's witchcraft. It's a master weapon in satan's war room that takes on many forms. Did you know there are literally scores of different types of witchcraft practiced in the world, from better known forms like Santeria, Wicca, and Voodoo to obscure practices like Mama Chi, Kemetic, and Discordian. If you don't resist witchcraft, you're coming into agreement with it. I write more about this in my book, *Breaking Curses, Hexes, Vexes, Incantations, Potions and Spells.*

WITCHCRAFT IS REAL

Ephesians 6 speaks of principalities and powers. Principalities like Jezebel and Leviathan release a power—weaponized witchcraft. Witchcraft is satan's counterattack to the power of the Holy Spirit. Make no mistake, witchcraft is no match for the Spirit of God, but believers can fall prey to this weapon when they are in rebellion. First Samuel 15:23 says rebellion is as the sin of witchcraft. When we are not submitted to God, we are in rebellion. Instead of fleeing, when we rebel the enemy has an open door of attack.

Remember the church at Galatia? Paul rebuked them for opening the door to witchcraft. How did they open this door? Clearly, they were listening to the wrong voice. Galatians 3:1 recounts his words: "O foolish Galatians! Who has bewitched you that you should not obey the truth, before whose eyes Jesus Christ was clearly portrayed among you as crucified?" The New Living Translation says, "Who has cast an evil spell on you?" The Holman Christian Standard Bible says,

"Who has hypnotized you?" New Heart English Bible puts it this way: "Who has cunningly deceived you?"

Although it's clear the Galatians let Judaism enter into the church, the doctrine was flying in the face of the truth to put the church back in bondage to the law, which they were hopeless to keep. It was the enemy who sowed these seeds, albeit through people, and bewitched the believers. When we open the door to the enemy, he can bewitch our minds so we don't obey the truth. This is like demonic momentum because the more we fail to obey the truth, the wider the door of attack.

WHEN WITCHCRAFT ATTACKS YOU

When witchcraft attacks the mind, we lose sight of Jesus; we are more prone to sin. Witchcraft releases confusion against the mind, fatigue in the body, and more. I write about this in my book *Satan's Deadly Trio*. I heard the Lord say:

> *The spirit of witchcraft may attack you, but don't bow to it. Don't run into a cave and hide with the demonic imaginations attacking your mind. Don't repeat Elijah's mistake in running away from Jezebel after a great triumph. Know your enemy. Do not be ignorant of his devices. But know Me, the God of your victory. Stand and face the attack head-on and you will cast down witchcraft's swirl against your life. You will not fall.*

The enemy works to cloud your mind with witchcraft and skew your sensibilities. The enemy works to show you a cracked image of yourself in his cracked mirror. Set your mind and keep it set on things above. Keep your mind on Me rather than on yourself. Know and understand that you are always on My mind. My thoughts toward you are greater than the number of sand grains on the seashore. Not only is My mind on you, I have victory in mind for you. Embrace the mind of Christ even when and especially when the enemy wants to cloud your mind and show you wrong pictures of yourself.

NOTES

1. Rick Joyner, *Army of the Dawn, Part II* (Fort Mill, SC: MorningStar Publications, 2016).

2. Jill Austin, "A Vision for the New Year," IHOP Network, October 17, 2016, http://www.ihopnetwork.com/index .php/2016/10/17/jill-austin-a-vision-for-the-new-year.

3. Ibid.

4. David Wilkerson, *The Vision* (Pillar Books, 1975), 41.

5. A.A. Allen, "A Revival of the Devil's Witchcraft is Rising," https://youtu.be/2zGSOQA71M0.

CHAPTER 18

THE MYSTERY

OF SATAN'S WEAPONRY

S atan has no armor, but he does have weaponry. The Bible describes his weapons as fiery darts or flaming missiles. Paul points to this concept in Ephesians 6:16, encouraging us to lift up our shield of faith to quench all the fiery darts of the wicked one. Here's what I've learned: All darts are not created equal. Satan's fiery darts are filled with various flammable substances and set on fire. These darts are customized to strike your heart with red hot tips that steal your faith and set your life ablaze.

These darts can carry the fire of lust, the fire of fear, the fire of doubt, or any other raging fire that tempts to you come out of your seat in heavenly places and agree with the enemy's sinful suggestions. What many don't realize is these darts are often launched in the form of vain imaginations aimed at weaknesses in your soul. That's because the enemy can't get into your heart until he gets in your mind. Many years ago, the Holy Spirit put it to me this way—the battle is in the mind, but the war is for your heart.

Paul wrote these Holy Spirit-inspired words:

> *For though we walk in the flesh, we do not war after the flesh: (for the weapons of our warfare are not carnal, but mighty through God to the pulling down of strong holds;) casting down imaginations, and every high thing that exalteth itself against the knowledge of God, and bringing into captivity every thought to the obedience of Christ; and having in a readiness to revenge all disobedience, when your obedience is fulfilled* (2 Corinthians 10:3-6 KJV).

The New International Version calls the imaginations arguments and pretensions. Satan likes to debate with us in our minds until he wears us down. The New Living Translation calls these imaginations "proud obstacles." The New American Standard Bible deems them speculations. Other versions call them reasonings, reckonings, deceptive fantasies, and warped philosophies. That about covers it. Those are satan's fiery darts aimed at your thought life to deceive you, then tempt you into agreement with his dark ways so he can wreak havoc on your life.

SATAN'S LETHAL WEAPON

Some of satan's weaponry is more lethal than others. With that said, I've noticed a not-so-subtle spirit rising in the Body of Christ in the past few years. It's not-so-subtle to the one who is not under its attack, but its target often doesn't see the assignment until it's too late. That not-so-subtle spirit is offense.

I've been witnessing believers getting offended over slight corrections, unreturned phone calls, and even the way certain people say "Holy Spirit." I've heard about believers getting offended over new relationships forming, being asked to sit out travel trips, or not being invited into a back-room meeting.

The Spirit of God showed me clearly that these aren't immature, isolated incidents. There's an actual spirit rising that's causing these unreasonable offenses—and it's a sign of the times. It's satan's plot to divide believers in an hour of church history when it's more vital than perhaps ever before that we unite on our common beliefs.

Speaking of the end times, Jesus said, "And then many will be offended and repelled and will begin to distrust and desert [Him Whom they ought to trust and obey] and will stumble and fall away and betray one another and pursue one another with hatred" (Matt. 24:10 AMPC). *The Passion Translation* puts it this way: "Then many will stop following me and fall away, and they will betray one another and hate one another."

The Greek word for *offense* in that verse is *skandalizo*. (It sounds like *scandal* in English, doesn't it?) According to *The KJV New Testament Greek Lexicon*, it means "to entice to sin, to cause a person to begin to distrust and desert one whom he ought to trust and obey, to make indignant." We see the fruit of offense in Proverbs 18:19, "A brother offended is harder to win than a strong city, and contentions are like the bars of a castle."

People fall away from Christ, whom they should trust, when they get offended with Him. People walk away from churches over offense. People break relationships, quit jobs, stop supporting ministries, and more over offenses. The reality is, many if not most of the offenses are fueled by the devil's fiery darts—by imaginations, arguments, pretensions, proud obstacles, speculations, reasonings, reckonings, deceptive fantasies, and warped philosophies. Even when the offense is valid, the enemy's vain imaginations often blow the situation out of proportion. The weapon here—one of the most potent in the end times—is offense.

RUNNING RAMPANT IN THE CHURCH

I heard the Lord say:

> *A spirit of offense is rising and running rampant through the church. Those who are easily offended are candidates for the Great Falling Away. Those who cultivate and maintain an unoffendable heart will escape many of the assignments the enemy will launch in the days to come.*
>
> *For My people must band together in this hour and refuse to allow petty arguments and soulish imaginations separate them. This is the time to press into community and relationship and reject the demonic notions and wisdom the enemy is pouring out.*

The love of many is waxing cold. Brother is turning against brother and sister against sister—in My Body. You must come to the unity of the faith in order to accomplish what I've called you to do in this hour. The time is upon you. The opportunity is before you. Lay aside the resentment, bitterness, and unforgiveness and, as far as it depends upon you, seek peace with all men.

Humble yourselves even among those whom you feel are your enemies, and I will work to bring reconciliation that sets the scene for unity from which the anointing flows. You need My anointing to combat the antichrist spirits rising in this hour.

Many of My people are wrestling in their flesh, engaging in works of the flesh, and otherwise letting the flesh lead in battle—and they are battling flesh instead of the spirits influencing the flesh. This is the result of offense. Forgive, let go, embrace your brothers and sisters despite their flaws and sins. I have.

DON'T LET THIS WEAPON FORM

I see offense as this major weapon in the end-times battle for souls. The Bible says, "No weapon formed against you shall prosper" (see Isa. 54:17) in the context of the enemy forming weapons against us.

This is absolute truth. Unfortunately, many in the Body of Christ are not resisting the formation of this weapon, this fiery dart, this sinister voice of offense, and they put up no guard.

The spirit of offense that's running rampant in the church is causing much carnage in the Body. I liken it to an autoimmune disease. We've turned against ourselves. We are battling each other. We will have to root out the offense before we see the unified army rise. We will have to await the remnant who will cast offense down.

In times past, Holy Spirit poured out strategies for warfare, but they were ineffective because we didn't execute them due to offense with a pastor or other intercessor. We didn't go to the prayer meeting because someone cut us off last time. We stopped short of fulfilling the strategy because of personal pain, because of corporate pain, because someone broke rank and released friendly fire or pulled in the opposite direction out of rebellion or pride. A house divided cannot stand, and that's what the enemy is counting on. But we will stand.

Prophetically speaking, the remnant will outlast the offense and break through the betrayals. Once we stop battling each other and turn our mouths and our minds and our hearts toward defeating a common enemy, the strategies He's given us will actually work—and we will be able to sustain the victory. Jesus is coming back for a church without spot or wrinkle (see Eph. 5:26-27).

BATTLING THE SPIRIT OF OFFENSE

John Bevere has a classic book about offense called *The Bait of Satan*. I'd highly recommend picking up a copy in this hour, especially if you find yourself getting easily offended.

How can you tell if you are easily offended? Here are some markers: you are quick to argue and defend yourself; you are quick to anger; you get your feelings hurt easily; you keep playing comments or actions over and over in your mind and growing resentful; or you don't want to talk to a certain person anymore.

Again, offense is dangerous because "a brother offended is harder to win than a strong city, and contentions are like the bars of a castle" (Prov. 18:19). But love is not touchy or easily provoked (see 1 Cor. 13:5-6). We know that "good sense makes one slow to anger, and it is his glory to overlook an offense" (Prov. 19:11 ESV). And the preacher offers some really good advice: "Do not give heed to everything people say, lest you hear your servant cursing you. Your heart knows that many times you have spoken a curse against others" (Eccles. 7:21-22 MEV).

Ultimately, if you are offended the only way to escape that trap is to spit out the bait. Forgive. There are many, many Scriptures dealing with the forgiveness, which is a commandment, not an option. But here's one I'll leave you with: "You shall not take vengeance, nor bear any grudge against the children of your people, but you shall love your neighbor as yourself: I am the Lord" (Lev. 19:18 MEV).

Walk this way and you will walk free of offense—and avoid it altogether to begin with:

Love suffers long and is kind; love envies not; love flaunts not itself and is not puffed up, does not behave itself improperly, seeks not its own, is not easily provoked, thinks no evil; rejoices not in iniquity, but rejoices in the truth; bears all things, believes all things, hopes all things, and endures all things (1 Corinthians 13:4-7 MEV).

Amen.

16 WAYS TO DISCERN AN OFFENDED HEART

I've discovered there are telltale signs of an offended heart—and the ultimate root of offense is pride. However, we may not recognize those signs in our life or the lives of others because they are often subtle or we are already blinded to it.

1. Big complainers. We all complain from time to time, but someone with an offended heart complains more than most. They complain about what people do or say to them—or don't do or say to them. They complain about the way others behave or what they receive. They complain about something most of the time.

2. Condemning critics. Beyond complaining about behaviors, people with an offended heart grow critical of the actual person. As this advances, the offended heart criticizes their targets for things they didn't even do or say based on their own twisted perceptions of reality.

3. Attention-seekers. People with an offended heart want your attention. They believe a lie that tells them they can demand your attention with evil reports about others. This, of course, elevates them to a position of importance in their own mind. Remember, offense is rooted in pride.

4. Insecurity abounds. People with an offended heart have a measure of insecurity, which is often connected to pride. Insecure people speak ill of others behind their backs, again to elevate themselves. They don't feel safe or secure in who they are, so they have to attack others to make them feel comfortable in their own skin.

5. Victimhood rises. People with an offended heart usually have a string of sad stories about how people have wronged them. They may have been genuinely hurt and wounded, but now they see everything through the lens of victimhood whether they are being treated unfairly or not.

6. Pity parties frequent. People with an offended heart want your pity, which is connected with victimhood. They hope you will take up their offense and give them special treatment because of the injustice they've endured. Beware of taking up another person's offense. It's dangerous.

7. Playing the blame game. People with an offended heart blame other people for their emotions, situations, and circumstances. They don't take responsibility for their own feelings but instead point fingers. Blame is the guard to change.

8. Trigger-happy. People with an offended heart are easily triggered into a new offense. They are hyper-sensitive to anything that looks or sounds offensive and are vulnerable to tapping into imaginary offenses the devil orchestrates to keep them in bondage.

9. Operate in presumption. People with an offended heart operate in presumption instead of truth. They automatically believe the worst instead of believing the best.

10. Strife-spreaders. People with an offended heart won't go to the person who offended them but will tell everybody else what someone did to them. This is dangerous according to Matthew 18, but it's especially dangerous when it's based in false perceptions. Sowing discord among brethren is an abomination to the Lord (see Prov. 6:19).

11. Negative Nancys. People with an offended heart have an overall negative bent to them. They are quick to speak, quick to judge, and slow to see the good in people or circumstances. They only believe the best of those who haven't offended them—yet.

12. Fleeing spirit. People with an offended heart will not respond to your requests for reconciliation. They will avoid you, ignore you, and otherwise refuse to engage in a conversation that could bring clarity and freedom.

13. Manipulating and controlling. People with an offended heart will begin manipulating situations to set people up for a fall. If you offend them, they will work to get others to rise up against you.

14. Quick to anger. People with an offended heart are quick to anger. It's unreasonable anger.

15. Narcissistic tendencies. People with an offended heart cannot be confronted with facts. You can't reason with them because the spirit of offense is unreasonable.

16. Unforgiving, resentful, and bitter. People with an offended heart have a root of bitterness, and resentment is evident in their conversation. They have ought in their soul and refuse to let go of the bait of satan.

CHAPTER 19

BUILDING
YOUR WAR ROOM ON EARTH

Doubtless you've seen the blockbuster Christian movie *War Room*. Back in 2015, the film sent the masses back to their prayer closets with renewed determination to defeat the devil. People around the world peppered their walls with Scriptures and photos as part of a multimillion-dollar trend in the Body of Christ.

My concept of a war room is similar, but also somewhat different. My war room is not for mere intercessors looking for a quiet place to pray with Scripture references surrounding them as weaponized prompts. Based on my epic vision, my war room is a fully equipped situation room to strategize even before intercession takes place.

Although you can't find the phrase "war room" in the Bible, war rooms are scriptural. In fact, for all the attention—and with due purpose—on the throne room, we have largely left other rooms in heaven unexplored. The Bible speaks specifically of upper rooms and gives us a hint as to the purpose of these rooms—prayer.

Amos 9:6 shows us, "He builds His upper rooms in the heavens and founds His vault upon the earth. He summons the waters of the sea and pours them over the face of the earth. The Lord is His name" (BSB). We can build our upper room, our prayer closet, our war room—a place where we hear His voice and lift up prayer in response to His will—and we should.

DANIEL'S UPPER ROOM

Daniel gives us our first glimpse of an upper room as a prayer room—or a war room. Daniel was the object of jealousy because he distinguished himself above his contemporaries and had an excellent spirit. The governors and satraps plotted against him by convincing King Darius to sign a royal statute indicating whoever petitions any god or man besides the king would be thrown into a den of lions. This is when Daniel's upper room—his prayer room—became a war room. Daniel 6:10 tells us:

> *Now when Daniel knew that the writing was signed, he went home. And in his upper room, with his windows open toward Jerusalem, he knelt down on his knees three times that day, and prayed and gave thanks before his God, as was his custom since early days.*

The fiery darts—the vain imaginations—about his fate must have been raging. I believe Daniel did battle in prayer before he walked into the den. I believe God strengthened him to walk into the lion's den by faith while on his knees in the war room.

The upper room is a place of prayer—and at times a place of war. Jesus said, "But you, when you pray, go into your room, and when you have shut your door, pray to your Father who is in the secret place; and your Father who sees in secret will reward you openly" (Matt. 6:6). Of course, the Book of Acts records the prayer meeting that set the stage for the birth of the New Testament church. Acts 1:12-14 reads:

> *Then they returned to Jerusalem from the mount called Olivet, which is near Jerusalem, a Sabbath day's journey. And when they had entered, they went up into the upper room where they were staying: Peter, James, John, and Andrew; Philip and Thomas; Bartholomew and Matthew; James the son of Alphaeus and Simon the Zealot; and Judas the son of James. These all continued with one accord in prayer and supplication, with the women and Mary the mother of Jesus, and with His brothers.*

You know what happens next. The Holy Spirit entered the upper room with the sound like a mighty rushing wind and filled the place. Divided tongues like fire landed on each one and they got a new prayer language. Catch that! The disciples received a new prayer language in the upper room (see Acts 2:1-4). People of prayer are more likely to see the rooms in heaven because they spend much time speaking the language of heaven. Indeed, prayer—all manner of prayer—is a gateway to the seer dimensions. Jesus said, "Watch and pray" (Matt. 26:41). But He could just as easily have said pray and watch.

YOUR SECRET WAR ROOM

You can pray and watch for Jehovah Gibbor's battle plan while praying in your war room, which should be your own secret place. Churches or houses of prayer may have public war rooms, but your war room needs to be personal to you as many of your battles you will fight alone. Jesus said:

> *And when you pray, you shall not be like the hypocrites. For they love to pray standing in the synagogues and on the corners of the streets, that they may be seen by men. Assuredly, I say to you, they have their reward. But you, when you pray, go into your room, and when you have shut your door, pray to your Father who is in the secret place; and your Father who sees in secret will reward you openly* (Matthew 6:5-6).

I believe when we pray in our secret war room, the Lord rewards us with open victory. The Greek word for *room* in that verse is *tameion*. It means an inner chamber or a secret room, according to *The KJV New Testament Greek Lexicon*. It's like the Situation Room in the White House in that what is shared there is confidential information about pressing situations. Consider Luke 12:3: "Therefore whatever you have spoken in the dark will be heard in the light, and what you have spoken in the ear in inner rooms will be proclaimed on the housetops." There's a time to receive prophetic intelligence in the secret room. You shout it from the rooftops when you enter into war.

In a perfect world, our war room would look just like Jehovah's war room. Because we have so little revelation of what the war room in heaven really looks like—we know in part and we prophesy in part (see 1 Cor. 13:9)—I can only share with you how I built my war room. While your war room doesn't have to look exactly like mine, you can draw from my experience and adapt the concept to fit your situation.

Your time in the war room is the calm before the storm. It's your quiet time with God before you go toe to toe with the devil. It is where you are still, knowing Him as Jehovah Gibbor. It is where you look to the Lord and His strength and seek His face (see 1 Chron. 16:11). It is where you draw near to God, and He draws near to you (see James 4:8). It is where you meditate on His word so you can find success in the battle like Joshua (see Josh. 1:8).

LOCATE YOUR WAR ROOM

My war room is not in a closet, though yours can be. Your war room just needs to be a place dedicated to study and prayer that's clearly distinguished from the rest of your home. It's consecrated—set apart—for this particular use. Your war room should be in a private place with minimal distraction from family and friends. If you can't pray in a room, get a wall divider to section off an area for prayer.

INVEST IN A PRAYER CHAIR

I have a prayer chair—a bright orange prayer chair. The chair is designated for prayer. It's not a chair for chatting on the phone or watching TV. The chair is set apart and there is an anointing that rests on that chair. I put a mantle Chuck Pierce gave me over the back of the chair. While you war standing up (or sometimes on your knees), you can strategize sitting down. Part of your war strategy will come through Bible study and meditation on the Word. You'll need a chair.

OPEN YOUR WAR CHEST

Your war room is beyond a prayer closet because there's equipment in the war room. I have a war chest. Beyond my spiritual weapons, I have an arsenal that includes books on spiritual warfare, various lexicons and Bible translations, and some ear plugs. Why the ear plugs? It helps me cut off the outside world with all the noises that would distract me.

My war chest includes my personal book of revelation with what the Lord has showed me in the past. Because we fight with the Word of God, it's important to surround yourself with materials you can tap into to help you study through what the Lord is showing you or make intercession. You may also want to keep some music in your war chest. Sometimes music helps you calm and quiet your soul so that you can hear what the Lord is saying about the fight you are in.

KEEP PEN AND PAPER HANDY

A war room is a place where you receive revelation of the enemy's plans. Therefore, the responsible warrior keeps a pen and paper—or some sort of digital device—on which you can scribe the strategies and tactics the Holy Spirit reveals to you about the specific battle you fighting. Don't assume you will remember everything He says.

God told Moses to write down things He said as a permanent reminder (see Exod. 17:14). God told Jeremiah to write all the things He said in a book (see Jer. 30:2). Yes, the Holy Spirit can remind you, but a strategic warrior writes the vision for victory God gives him so others can run with it. You need a battle plan. In my devotional book, *Victory Decrees: Daily Prophetic Strategies for Spiritual Warfare Victory*, I penned these prophetic words from the Holy Spirit:

> Just as Father was with Jesus, He is with you. And your Father in heaven is a master strategist. No enemy attack takes Him by surprise. No whispered lie the wicked one releases convinces Him to leave you. Yes, the devil is the Accuser of the Brethren and he accuses you to Father. He accuses Father to you. He accuses you to yourself and he causes you to look for someone to blame for your warfare. Don't fall into this demonic trap. Turn to your Father in heaven for a strategy of war that will surprise the enemy of your soul. You cannot lose.

DECORATE THE WAR ROOM

If you have the space, put up a cork board or find a space on the wall where you can put up sticky notes. Sticky notes are the prayer warrior's friend. You can write down phrases that inspire you, names of people to pray for, or Scriptures. I have a map in my war room, because some of my intercession involves the nations. The idea is to inspire yourself to keep pressing so you don't grow weary in well doing.

TAP INTO TECHNOLOGY

Just like the Situation Room in the White House has high-tech bells and whistles, my war room uses technology to advance in the battle. I have my laptop ready to research anything the Lord shows me that I can't quickly find in a book. I have my smartphone ready to dictate visions that happen too fast to write down as they are unfolding before my very spiritual eyes. Technology can be a tool if you use it tactically. Be careful you don't wander off into social media land during your war room sessions. The enemy wants to distract you.

INVITE THE ANGELS TO THE TABLE

In my vision, I saw angels at the table in God's war room. Angels of revelation hang out in my war room. Remember, angels hearken to the voice of God's Word. Invite the angels to the table to listen in so when you start decreeing the word of the Lord, they are ready to war in the spirit with you.

The war room is a secret place where you receive prophetic intelligence from heaven. Angels ascend and descend with revelation, like unto Jacob's dream in Genesis 12. It's not a place for corporate warfare; rather, it's a secret place where you run into the strong tower and find safety and strategy.

Keep in mind you won't do all your warfare in your war room. Although I do warfare in my war room, again, it's just as much about equipping myself and getting strategy as it is engaging in battle. Sometimes you have to set up a makeshift war room, like Elisha in Second Kings 4:33. When the child of his friend died, the bedroom became a war room.

ABOUT
JENNIFER LECLAIRE

Jennifer LeClaire is senior leader of Awakening House of Prayer in Fort Lauderdale, Florida, founder of the Ignite Network, and founder of the Awakening Prayer Hubs prayer movement. Jennifer formerly served as the first-ever female editor of *Charisma* magazine and is a prolific author of over 50 books. You can find Jennifer online or shoot her an email at info@jenniferleclaire.org.

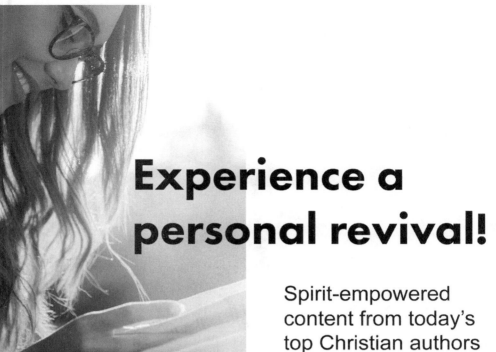